Buffalo Bill pictured in 1903 around the time of his first performance in Essex

This book is dedicated to my wife, Anne, for her help and encouragement.

DAVID DUNFORD

BUFFALO BILL'S WILD WEST

THE FIRST REALITY SHOW IN ESSEX

Essex Hundred Publications
Rutland House
90 – 92 Baxter Avenue
Southend-on-Sea
Essex SS2 6HZ
www.essex100.com

BUFFALO BILL'S WILD WEST
The First Reality Show in Essex
First published October 2018
David Dunford
© David Dunford
October 2018
Reprinted July 2019
Reprinted March 2022

All rights reserved.

No part of this book may be reprinted or reproduced or utilised in any form or by any electronic, mechanical or other means, now known or hereafter invented, including photocopying and recording, or in any information storage or retrieval system, without the permission in writing from the publishers.
British library cataloguing in Publication Data.

A catalogue record for this book is available from
The British Library
ISBN 9780993108389
Typeset by Hutchins Creative Limited
Printed by 4edge Publishing
22 Eldon Way
Eldon Way Industrial Estate
Hockley Essex SS5 4AD

Contents

Page 6	Acknowledgements
Page 7	List of Illustrations
Page 9	Introduction
Page 11	1. The Making of a Legend
Page 19	2. Treading the Boards
Page 27	3. The Wild West Show is Born
Page 33	4. The Early Years – Annie Oakley and Sitting Bull
Page 43	5. The Wild West Arrives in Essex
Page 49	6. The American Exhibition
Page 61	7. Across the Atlantic Again
Page 67	8. On the Road
Page 71	9. Three Days in September – Leyton, Southend and Colchester
Page 87	10. The Final Tour – Chelmsford and Ilford
Page 97	11. The End of the Trail
Page 106	Selected Bibliography
Page 108	About the Author
Page 109	Essex Hundred Publications

Acknowledgements

My thanks are due to:-
Newsquest Essex Basildon for unrestricted access to the newspaper's archives. Steven Gardner at Waltham Forest Archive and Local Studies Library for his enthusiastic help in navigating through reels of microfilm. Essex County Library staff at Colchester and Grays. The staff at Essex Record Office in Chelmsford. Dr Marie-Paule Powell, Professor Emeritus University of Toronto, for her comments and careful proof reading.

List of Illustrations

*Images on the cover and frontispiece and pages
8, 11, 13, 14, 16, 18, 19, 22, 23, 25, 26, 28, 29, 30, 32, 35, 37, 40, 41, 42, 44, 60, 71, 74, 78, 83, 88, 91, 96, 98, 99, 100, 102 and 105 are courtesy of US Library of Congress*

Image on page 58 from the Pall Mall Gazette May 1887

Image on page 59 from the Illustrated Sporting and Dramatic News May 1887

Image on page 64 from St James's Gazette December 1902

Image on page 68 from The Sphere January 1903

Images on pages 72 and 73 from the Illustrated Sporting and Dramatic News October 1903

Images on pages 34, 77, 80, 81, 84, 89, 93, 94 and 112 from the author's collection

Every effort has been made to contact copyright holders of images reproduced in this book. If any have been inadvertently overlooked the publisher will be pleased to make restitution at the earliest opportunity

Poster for Buffalo Bill's Wild West from the period when the show visited Essex

Introduction

At the beginning of the twentieth century Colonel the Honourable William Frederick Cody, was one of the most famous men in the world. Better known as 'Buffalo Bill' he was an Indian fighter, army scout, buffalo hunter, Pony Express rider and hero of countless dime novels. He had been a friend of Wild Bill Hickock and as a twelve-year-old met Kit Carson. He was, therefore, an unlikely figure to be found on the streets of several Essex towns in 1903 and 1904. The reason lay in his other great talent; he was above all a brilliant showman and had been the star of his own Wild West show for nearly twenty years.

His show was no circus. Forty years before Lord Reith decreed the BBC should inform, educate and entertain, Cody adopted the same principals. The men and women who took part had often been involved in the actual incidents they portrayed. It was, in effect, the world's first reality show. More than a hundred years before the idea became ubiquitous on television and typified by 'The Only Way is Essex', Buffalo Bill brought his own reality show to the county. Cody's Wild West (the word 'show' was never used in publicity) was astounding, featuring hundreds of performers, horses and animals. In the mid 1880s, just nine years after the Battle of the Little Big Horn which saw the massacre of General George Custer and his 7th Cavalry, Sitting Bull – the leader of the victorious Sioux – toured with it for four months. In 1891 the Wild West came to Britain with twenty three Indian prisoners of war who had been released to Buffalo Bill's care after an uprising. Later, troops who had taken part re-enacted the Battle of San Juan Hill which was fought during the Spanish-American War in Cuba. The cowboys had actually ridden the range, the cavalry men were real veterans and the Indians were real Indians. When the show first visited Britain in 1887, as part of the American Exhibition in London, the catalogue proclaimed: 'No exhibition of "America in miniature" would be complete without a faithful representation of the conditions of life in the far West'. Buffalo Bill's Wild West was 'designed to illustrate the life of the frontiersman and the North American Indian and to graphically portray the methods by which the United States have been civilised, from Atlantic to Pacific coast. It must be distinctly borne in mind that this representation is given by real people, who have been brought five thousand miles from their prairie homes, and by Indians taken from their reservations by permission of the United States Government.'

The *Illustrated London News* agreed: 'It is not a circus, nor indeed is it acting at all, in a theatrical sense; but an exact reproduction of daily scenes in frontier life, as experienced and enacted by the very people who now form the "Wild West" Company'

In 1892, when the Wild West was asked to perform for Queen Victoria at Windsor Castle, her son-in-law, Prince Henry of Battenburg, expressed some scepticism to the Queen about the authenticity of what they had seen. Buffalo Bill's long-time partner, Nate Salsbury, turned to the Queen and said: 'I beg to assure you ... that everything and everybody you see in the entertainment are exactly what we represent them to be.'

Over the years the Wild West grew and grew. By the time the show came to Essex for the first time there were 800 staff and performers; the travelling arena could accommodate more than 12,000 spectators and it had added many circus sideshows. All this required three special trains to transport around the country. But despite this, the Wild West was still firmly rooted in Buffalo Bill's ideas of authenticity. Shortly before it arrived in Southend in 1903, Bill's partner and publicity chief, Major John Burke, assured the newspaper that spectators would see actual people re-enacting historical incidents.

This is the story of Buffalo Bill, the Wild West and how more than a century before 'The Only Way is Essex' the county flocked to see the world's first reality show.

1. The Making of a Legend

William Frederick Cody was born in Le Claire, Iowa, on February 26th 1846, the fourth of eight children. Little is known about his mother, Mary Anne Leacock, except she was well educated and believed William would one day become president of the United States. He wasn't president but perhaps his mother would be surprised to learn that his name lives on even today when many American presidents of the nineteenth century are remembered only as footnotes to history.

The birthplace of Buffalo Bill. It originally stood in Le Claire, Iowa, but was later moved to the Buffalo Bill museum in Wyoming.

William may have inherited his drive and ambition from his father, Isaac Cody, a restless, energetic man who aspired to take his family to California. He had Irish blood and the first Codys had travelled to

America and settled in Massachusetts just one hundred years before William was born.

When William – known to his family as Will – was six tragedy struck the family. His brother, Samuel, was killed when he was thrown from a horse which reared and then fell backwards onto him. Mary Cody was so unhappy after the death of her son that her husband decided to move the family away from the scene of the fatal accident. They set off across Iowa with two large wagons carrying their worldly possessions. They journeyed for a month and young Will apparently enjoyed every minute, riding beside the wagons and pretending to be an Indian scout. They eventually made it to Kansas and the valley of Salt Creek. The original idea had been to continue moving westward to California and the newly discovered gold fields, but Isaac Cody liked the lush prairie of the Salt Creek valley and decided to settle there.

Isaac was against slavery and opposed those who wanted to extend it and his principles eventually led to his death. He got into an argument at a pro-slavery rally and was attacked and stabbed in the back. Incidents such as this were common in Kansas with those who supported slavery assaulting, tarring and feathering and even lynching those who opposed them. Although Isaac survived he was forced into hiding and his wife had difficulty running the small grocery store they'd bought with pro-slavery customers boycotting it. By the winter of 1854-55 the family was practically destitute. In the spring of 1857 Isaac finally felt he could return home but it appears he had never fully recovered from the stabbing three years before. In April he died and that meant the end of eleven-year-old Will's attendance at the one-roomed school house in Salt Creek.

After his father died, Will got occasional jobs herding cattle for settlers. He learned how to survive in the hostile and often violent frontier world. Handling horses and guns became second nature.

Even at the age of eleven Will Cody was a striking figure. He had big brown eyes, fine features and a mop of blonde hair. He was a good rider, a crack shot and the principal breadwinner for his family of six. Will persuaded his mother to let him take a job with a company shipping freight westward by wagon train. These wagon trains may well have given him ideas he later used to such effect when moving his Wild West show around on tour.

A typical wagon train consisted of twenty five big covered wagons or 'prairie schooners' each drawn by twelve oxen. They were followed by twenty or thirty extra oxen in case of accidents or lameness. At its head was a wagon master or his assistant followed by a team of men. These were followed in turn by a man to look after the extra oxen and several more men in reserve. They travelled twelve to fifteen miles a day and sometimes twenty. To operate efficiently the train needed organisation and discipline with each individual doing his job to perfection. Any confusion meant delay. It was a lesson Will was to carry with him into the organisation of his Wild West show many years later.

His job with the wagon train was as a messenger taking dispatches from one wagon to another. Like every other employee he was obliged to sign a pledge agreeing not to use profane language, not to get drunk, gamble, or treat animals cruelly.

The cavalry barracks at Fort Laramie in Wyoming photographed in the 1930s. It was here Will Cody first met the famous scouts Kit Carson and Jim Bridger.

Although it's unproved, Will claimed he killed his first Indian on his first trip. He said later he was tired and lagging behind the wagon train when he saw an Indian silhouetted against the moon, he raised his old muzzle loading rifle and fired. Whether it was true or not, the story was picked up by a newspaper and Will acquired a reputation as 'the youngest Indian slayer of the plains.'

On another trip he stopped at Fort Laramie in Wyoming where he came across the famous scouts Kit Carson and Jim Bridger who made an immediate impression on the twelve-year-old.

Wild Bill Hickok: Will Cody rode with him at the age of just fourteen

From them he picked up a working knowledge of the Sioux language and the ambition to become a frontier scout. There followed an unsuccessful season as a trapper during which he broke his leg and had to wait alone, snowed in and surrounded by wolves, for twenty nine days for rescue. After that Will secured a job on the newly opened Pony Express which could take messages across the country from New York to San Francisco in ten days. It was a mammoth undertaking: between 400 and 500 horses were needed with 190 stations, 200 station keepers and eighty riders. Each rider averaged just under thirty miles riding three ponies in relays at full gallop, although in emergencies they could do greater distances.

On one occasion, as Will was setting out from a station, fifteen Indians tried to catch him. He dug in his spurs, lay flat on the pony's back and outran them. There was more drama on another journey when he galloped into a station to find the next rider had been killed in a fight the night before. Will promptly changed mounts and continued eighty five miles to the next station. He then turned back and rode to his starting point making the 320-mile trip in twenty one hours and forty minutes. Later, the by then fourteen-year-old Will was to take part in a raid with Wild Bill Hickok on a party of Indians who had been stealing Pony Express horses. It was an exciting period but rapid development of the telegraph made the Pony Express obsolete in less than sixteen months and it ended in October 1861.

As one opportunity for adventure closed another opened: the American Civil War was six months old when Will Cody found himself out of a job. Will was only fifteen and talked of enlisting in the Union Army but his mother begged him not to and he took a succession of temporary jobs. In 1863 his mother died and in 1864, aged eighteen, he enlisted in the Seventh Kansas Regiment.

Soon after, his regiment was sent to Tennessee where he was ordered to scout Confederate positions. In what was probably his first theatrical role he adopted the disguise of a Tennessee farm boy and affected a southern accent. Later while serving as a hospital orderly in St. Louis he met Louisa Frederici; they fell in love and decided to marry. But before embarking on married life Will had to earn some money and after being discharged from the army he took a job as a stagecoach driver. The couple finally married in March 1866 in St Louis. Louisa was unhappy with Will's lifestyle and reluctantly he promised he would abandon the western plains and mountains and settle down – a promise he could not keep. He set himself up in the hotel business but although he was a good host, the scale of his generosity prevented him making the job a success. Finding he wasn't suited to the hotel business, Will moved to Kansas where he again met Wild Bill Hickok who told him the army needed scouts. He was recruited and found himself serving under the command of General George Armstrong Custer. After this, he found a job supplying meat to the railroad builders who were moving westwards and which made his reputation as a buffalo killer and earned him his nickname. In seventeen months Will killed 4,280 buffalo and from that time on he was known as 'Buffalo Bill'. From buffalo hunting Bill took a job with the army and distinguished himself by carrying important dispatches several times through territory occupied by hostile Indians. It was at this period Bill was to take part in an action which years later he re-enacted in his Wild West show. He rode with five companies of the 5th Cavalry to deal with a band of Cheyenne, led by Chief Tall Bull, who were raiding settlements, killing civilians and abducting women. During the course of the ensuing battle Bill shot Tall Bull from a range of less than thirty yards.

Soon after this, Buffalo Bill began the transformation from frontiersman to global celebrity. He began leading groups of the rich and distinguished on buffalo hunts. This gave him access to the upper echelons of society in New York where he was introduced to a dime novel writer, E.Z.C. Judson, who wrote under the name Ned Buntline. As well as writing, Buntline was an adventurer, actor and promoter who lived by his wits. He was a drunkard who delivered temperance lectures as a side line; always broke, always in trouble, he was often in jail. Legend has it that later in his career he commissioned the arms manufacturer Colt to make a revolver with an extra-long barrel – the famous 'Buntline Special' two of which he presented to Wyatt Earp and Bat Masterson in Dodge City. Despite his many adventures, in 1869 Buntline had run out of material which he could turn into lurid fiction and was looking for a hero for his stories; in Buffalo Bill he found his man. Almost overnight Buntline made Cody famous with a story in the *New York Weekly* entitled 'Buffalo Bill, The King of the Border Men.' It was the first of many tales in which Bill was glorified and which cemented his place in the minds

Ned Buntline: Dime novel writer who brought fame to Buffalo Bill

of millions of people. Buffalo Bill Cody was famous at the age of just twenty three.

Three years later, one of Buntline's stories was adapted for the stage in New York and on a visit to the city Buffalo Bill and Buntline went to see it. Bill's part was played by a versatile and popular actor named J.B. Studley whose performance had been well received by the critics. One wrote that the audience were spellbound and as the plot unfolded, climaxing in the victory of Buffalo Bill over his adversaries, 'the burst of enthusiasm that followed would have rivalled the roar of Niagara'. It seems to have been a lightbulb moment for Bill Cody sitting in the audience. He had already seen a world of wealth and splendour, luxury and pleasure through his contacts with the people he led on fashionable hunting expeditions; he was a celebrity thanks to the novels of Ned Buntline. Now he realised that if Buntline could make money by exploiting him, he could make money by exploiting himself. At first, he was reluctant to take up acting but eventually he changed his mind when he was offered 500 dollars a week to play himself on stage – four times what he ever earned hunting buffalo.

Before he could take up the offer, Bill was summoned back out west to help fight more hostile Indians. Buntline planned to write a stage play which would be put on in Chicago and Bill promised to return to take part and bring some Indians with him.

During this trip west there was a brief skirmish during which Bill suffered a head wound – the only time he was wounded in battle. Shortly after this Bill was recommended for the Congressional Medal of Honour and he was also notified that he had been elected to the Nebraska State Legislature. Although he never took his seat, he seized on the opportunity to use the title 'Honourable' before his name – which he did for the rest of his life. Meanwhile, Ned Buntline wrote to remind Bill of his promise to appear on stage in Chicago. Bill returned not with the agreed twenty Indians but with a fellow scout he'd met on the plains, Texas Jack Omohundro. Buntline was unworried and proposed hiring ten out of work actors and dressing them up as

Indians. Whatever problems he faced, Buntline retained a cheerful optimism and when, unhappy at the non-appearance of real Indians, the theatre manager demanded to see the play's script Buntline confessed he hadn't actually written it.

The manager was horrified – this was Thursday; the opening was on Monday.

Buffalo Bill was still in his early twenties when the writer Ned Buntline made him famous as the hero of a series of dime novels. This lithograph dates from that period

2. Treading the Boards

Buntline booked Bill, Texas Jack and himself into cheap hotel rooms and set about writing the play. He boasted later it took him four hours – much of it was plagiarised from the New York play which had originally fired Bill's interest in the theatre.

Buffalo Bill's stage debut came in December 1872 when he was twenty six. The play was called 'Scouts of the Plains', it starred Buffalo Bill, Texas Jack and Ned Buntline as three scouts with an Italian American actress named Giuseppina Morlacchi in the only female role – Dove Eye, an Indian maiden.

Ned Buntline, Buffalo Bill Cody, Giuseppina Morlacchi and Texas Jack Omohundro in 'Scouts of the Plains'

The first night was a sell-out and the curtain rose to reveal the scouts dressed in fringed buckskin standing nervously behind the footlights. The opening line belonged to Bill but now as he stared out at the packed audience he couldn't remember a word of it. Buntline quickly came to the rescue and asked Bill about a recent hunting expedition and the question prompted him to start a description of what had happened. The script was rapidly abandoned and Texas Jack and Buntline managed to keep Bill talking. The problem came when it was time to bring down the curtain on the first act. Finally, Buntline signalled into the wings for the 'Indians'. They came screeching onto the stage to be met by a barrage of gunfire from the scouts.

The second act made some attempt to revert to the script and the third consisted of more shooting as the Indians were resurrected and attacked again. The critics hated it, one speaking of 'incongruous dialogue' and 'execrable acting'. But despite that, this largely improvised entertainment was a massive hit. More importantly it gave Bill the idea that, certainly where the Wild West was concerned, the audience wanted 'reality' rather than acting. The show set out on tour from Chicago and was a success wherever it played. The more the cast extemporised the more the audience loved it. The critics remained bemused; one wrote: 'The whole performance was so far outside of human experience, so wonderful in its daring feebleness, that no ordinary intellect is capable of comprehending it'. Another said Bill was a good looking fellow but 'ridiculous as an actor'. Finally, a writer for the *New York World* saw the potential in this new form of entertainment: 'As a drama it is very poor slop but as an exhibition of three remarkable men it is not without interest. The Hon. W.F. Cody enters into the spectacle with a curious grace and a certain characteristic charm that pleases the beholders. He is a remarkably handsome fellow on the stage and the lithe, springy step, the round western voice, the utter absence of anything like stage art, won for him the good will of an audience that was disposed to laugh at all that was intended to be pathetic and serious'.

Shortly after the play opened Buntline was arrested for jumping bail many years before and his receipts from 'Scouts of the Plains' were threatened with seizure. He avoided this by simply changing the name of the play to 'Scouts of the Prairie' with a fictitious ownership and management and the tour continued.

Despite the success of the production, Bill was disappointed with his share of the profits and decided that Buntline was not the man to manage him. He joined forces, instead, with 'Arizona John' Burke, a former character actor who had done virtually every job in the theatre and worked occasionally on newspapers. Burke liked to style himself as 'Major' although it's not clear whether or where he held that rank. Friends said he had 'nothing but brass and wind as his stock in trade' but he was a popular man and his press contacts became an important element in the promotion of Buffalo Bill. He was to use for the first time many publicity methods which are common today including celebrity endorsements, press kits, publicity stunts, newspaper articles, billboards and product licensing. Burke had the imagination to see how Bill could dominate show business. In their first season together they signed Wild Bill Hickok to replace Ned Buntline in the 'Scouts of the Prairie'.

Hickok had attempted to run an early Wild West show and the resulting disaster was to provide a valuable lesson in what not to do when Buffalo Bill set out on his own venture. Hickok's show involved Indians and wild buffalo and the opening was set for Niagara Falls in 1870. The idea failed spectacularly as he had not solved the logistics of presenting the show outdoors and charging admission. As the Indians tried to herd buffalo into the arena they made a break for freedom and had to be pursued through the streets. Even worse, a grizzly bear which was part of a sideshow got loose from its cage. Eventually Wild Bill had to sell the buffalo in order to raise enough money to get the Indians and himself home to the plains.

Hickok's skill as an actor was little better than his talent as an entrepreneur. He would amuse himself by firing blanks at the legs of other actors to make them jump and demanded real whisky rather than the stage version of cold tea.

In order to encourage him to behave Buffalo Bill decided to provide him with the real thing. Unfortunately, this tended to make Hickok amorous and he became fonder of the heroine on stage than was required by the script. Eventually he grew bored and left the play.

Under John Burke's management Buffalo Bill finally made money and although he still longed for the west he realised he would have to spend more time in the east. Accordingly, he moved his family to Rochester, New York, where in 1876 he suffered the greatest personal tragedy in his life – the death from scarlet fever of his six-year-old son Kit. A broken-hearted Bill resumed touring with his show, but a few weeks later embarked on his last great adventure as a western scout. He was asked by the army to return to help deal with the Indian uprising which was to culminate in the massacre of General George Custer and the 7th Cavalry at the battle of the Little Big Horn in June 1876. Following the battle, Buffalo Bill was acting as Chief Scout for the 5th Cavalry when they came upon a large band of two or three hundred Indians making their way to join the Sioux led by Sitting Bull who were the victors of the Little Big Horn. During the ensuing skirmish Bill shot and killed a Cheyenne Chief named Yellow Hand at close range.

George Armstrong Custer. Buffalo Bill avenged his death by killing Chief Yellow Hand.

An artist's impression of the scalping of Yellow Hand

Accounts of what happened vary greatly but Bill himself later wrote that one of the Indians, who was handsomely decorated with all the ornaments usually worn by a war chief when engaged in a fight, called out in his own tongue: 'I know you Pa-he-haska (long hair). If you want to fight, come ahead and fight me'. Bill added: 'The chief was riding his horse back and forth in front of his men, as if to banter me, and I concluded to accept the challenge. I galloped towards him fifty yards and he advanced towards me about the same distance, both of us riding at full speed. And then, when we were only thirty yards apart, I raised my rifle and fired; his horse fell to the ground having been killed by my bullet. Almost at the same time my own horse went down, he having stepped into a hole. The fall did not hurt me much and I sprang to my feet. The Indian had also recovered himself, and we were now both on foot, and now not more than twenty paces apart. We fired at each other simultaneously. My usual luck did not desert me on this occasion, for his bullet missed me, while mine struck him in the breast. He reeled and fell, but before he had fairly touched the ground, I was upon him, knife in hand, and had driven the keen-edged weapon into his heart. Jerking his war bonnet off, I scientifically scalped him ...'

Raising the bloody scalp in the air, Buffalo Bill shouted the words which were to become famous: 'First Scalp for Custer'. Whatever the truth of this encounter – at one stage Bill himself dismissed it as 'Bunk! Pure bunk. For all I know Yellow Hand died of old age' – Buffalo Bill returned to the stage a hero in the autumn of 1876; his show now containing a melodramatic re-enactment of his duel with Yellow Hand. He also displayed the fallen warrior's scalp, feather war bonnet, knife, saddle and other personal effects.

Later his Wild West show often contained a similar large-scale recreation of the scene entitled 'The Red Right Hand, or, Buffalo Bill's First Scalp for Custer'. It should be noted that while the practice of scalping is often associated with the Indians, it was primarily the white man who promoted it. Originally early colonial governments paid a bounty to friendly Indians for the scalps of enemies. Eventually Indians abandoned scalping but the white man on the frontier continued it with enthusiasm and it was looked on as no more appalling than the mounting of heads or tails of wild animals shot for sport.

Bill returned east a hero once more and went back on the road with John Burke and 'Scouts of the Prairie'. But he was now obsessed with a new idea – he wanted to move beyond a mere stage show. He wanted to recreate for everyone all the colour, action and excitement he had known in the west.

The only survivor of the Battle of the Little Big Horn was a horse named Commanche

A contemporary print showing Custer's death struggle. The Battle of the Little Big Horn took place on June 25th 1876 and the precise details are still a matter for debate today, more than 140 years later. What is known is that the battle was short and savage and resulted in an overwhelming victory for the Indians. Five of the 7th Cavalry's twelve companies were annihilated – 268 soldiers were killed and another fifty five were severely wounded of whom six later died of their injuries.

3. The Wild West Show is Born

Buffalo Bill's conviction that he could make a success of this new kind of spectacular show was driven by the continuing sales of the dime novels in which he featured and by the success of 'Scouts of the Prairie'. The show had spawned many imitators and there were similar productions in all the large cities. They all involved cowboys, Indians, scouts, a lost maiden to be rescued and some form of comic relief. The more shooting they contained the better the audience liked them. Buffalo Bill had to keep ahead of his competitors and it fell to John Burke, with his background in newspapers, to keep him in the public eye with a stream of articles, interviews, reviews and books.

The dime novels based on his adventures were now selling by the million and in between theatre tours Bill turned his hand to writing. In 1875 three of his stories were published in newspapers. Bill had little formal education and he was helped by his sister Helen as well as John Burke and Ned Buntline. Bill's literary output had little basis in fact but it added enormously to his legend. He wrote to one publisher: 'I am sorry to have to lie so outrageously in this yarn. My hero has killed more Indians on one war trail than I have killed in all my life. But I understand what is expected of border tales. If you think the revolver and the Bowie knife are used too freely, you may cut out the fatal shot or stab wherever you think wise.'

Buffalo Bill continued touring in a number of stage productions, all following the tried and tested formula. His biggest success came in the season of 1877-78 with 'May Cody, or Lost and Won'. One of Bill's friends, Gordon W. Lillie, later known as Pawnee Bill, who was working as an interpreter on an Indian reservation in Oklahoma, borrowed a number of Sioux for the show. Bill continued to tour and in the five years after his duel with Yellow Hand earned more than one hundred thousand dollars – worth more than two million today. But he saved almost none of it; he built a comfortable home in North Platte, Nebraska, which he called Welcome Wigwam where he could play the genial and generous host to his many friends. At the end of the 1881 season his wife, Louisa, met him in Omaha and caught her husband kissing goodbye to one of the company's actresses with more enthusiasm than she felt necessary. In an attempt to get back into Louisa's good books, he made the Nebraska property over to her – an action which prevented him borrowing money against it to raise capital for his planned Wild West show.

However, fate intervened. Around this time he was contacted by Nate Salsbury who was running a theatre company in New York. He was the same age as Cody and was one of the most successful actor-managers of his day. Salsbury was also working on ideas for a Wild West show and having studied Bill's life and career he'd decided Bill was the man to lead it. The two men met at a Brooklyn restaurant where they agreed the show had massive potential not only at home in America but also abroad. The only problem was funding it.

Nate Salsbury - one of the most successful actor-managers of his day

A few months later an opportunity arose. In June 1882 the citizens of North Platte decided to put on a show – to be called 'Old Glory Blow-Out' for the Fourth of July celebrations. Their original plan was for a rodeo but Bill persuaded them to back his idea of a Wild West show. He hired several Indians and bought the old Deadwood stagecoach with which he re-enacted a hold-up. The stagecoach was to become famous in its own right – featuring in every performance of the later Wild West show. It had once been pulled by six horses between Deadwood in South Dakota to Cheyenne via Laramie and War Bonnet Creek where Bill had killed Yellow Hand; a distance of around 270 miles. It was a substantial vehicle built to carry eighteen passengers – twelve inside and six on top as well as a driver and two men sitting beside him. The programme also included horse races, a sharp-shooting contest and the round-up of a small herd of buffalo; in short, the basic elements of the Buffalo Bill's Wild West show that would last for thirty years.

It was a tremendous success and Bill decided he would take it east. One of his neighbours, who took part in the show, was William Carver, known as Doc, a local dentist who claimed to be of Indian decent. He was an excellent trick shot and often took part in shooting contests at carnivals and county fairs. Gordon W. Lillie found some Pawnees and Major Frank North, who was a partner in Bill's Nebraska ranch, agreed to be billed as their 'White Chief'.

Doc Carver: A difficult partner

They hired local cowboys who could do lasso tricks and rope steers. They also recruited Captain Adam Bogardus, who called himself 'Champion Pigeon Shot of America' as a partner. Bogardus was an interesting character in his own right; at that time pigeon shooting meant just that – killing live passenger pigeons – and he had given his name to the 'Bogardus' rules which governed the matches in which contestants shot at pigeons released from traps. However, Bogardus deplored this slaughter and developed a system of spring traps throwing out glass balls to simulate live birds in flight. He was too late to stop the slaughter, however, which was also fuelled by the killing of millions of birds for the table. The last passenger pigeon died in Cincinnati Zoo in 1914.

For Buffalo Bill's show Bogardus restricted himself to clay pigeons. The show also included a Pony Express display and the old Deadwood Stagecoach. Major John Burke worked on the advance publicity and promotion. Bill wrote to Nate Salsbury inviting him to become a partner but when he heard that Doc Carver was involved he declined owing to a long-standing animosity between the two. One other member of the company was destined to remain with Buffalo Bill as long as he was in show business. This was Johnny Baker, who became known as 'The Cowboy Kid'. At the age of nine he would follow Buffalo Bill around in order to hold his horse and Bill – who always liked children – virtually adopted him. When the idea of the Wild West show was being

Captain Adam Bogardus

developed, Johnny, still in his early teens, begged to go along. After a winter of rehearsals, the show was ready for the road in the spring of 1883. The show was called 'The Wild West, Rocky Mountain and Prairie Exhibition' and opened at the fairgrounds in Omaha, Nebraska, on May 17th. Bill tried for the first time his later famous trick of shooting at glass balls tossed in the air – hitting eighty-seven out of a hundred – although it's thought the gun was loaded with lead shot which scattered rather than a single bullet; a technique he continued to use over the years.

Thus was born the show that would evolve into Buffalo Bill's Wild West – it was badly organised and crude in its production and with no artificial lighting it could be performed only once a day in daylight. The cowboys preferred to spend their time in saloons rather than performing and there were huge transport problems but the crowds loved it and reviews were enthusiastic. One newspaper reporter called it the 'best open-air show ever seen… The real sight of the whole thing is Buffalo Bill an extraordinary figure who sits on a horse as if he were born in the saddle. His feats of shooting are perfectly wonderful'.

Another reporter described the show saying the smell of gunpowder and cattle made it authentic: 'It began with a bareback riding race between Indians and went on to a climax with a grand realistic battle scene depicting the capture, torture and death of a scout by savages; the revenge, recapture of the dead body and victory of the government scouts. Cowboys rode bucking broncos, roped and tied Texas steers, lassoed and rode wild bison. A fleet footed Indian ran a race with a mounted rival. The Pony Express rider dashed in changed … to a fresh mount and dashed off again. The startling, soul-stirring attack on the Deadwood mail coach ended in rescue by Buffalo Bill and Dr. Carver.'

However good he may have been as a performer, Carver was difficult to work with and prone to violent rages when things went wrong. By the end of the season Bill was scarcely speaking to him. By chance Bill and Nate Salsbury met again in Chicago and Bill pleaded with him to join the show as a partner. As luck would have it, Dr. Carver announced he was ready to leave the show as he could no longer bear the strain of trying to manage the combination of cowboys, Indians, horses, cattle and buffalo. Salsbury then became a partner as did Bogardus and they began to make plans for the following year. Buffalo Bill's Wild West was on its way.

Although Buffalo Bill bought the original Deadwood stagecoach in 1882, the route itself continued until 1890. This picture shows the last trip

4. The Early Years – Annie Oakley and Sitting Bull

At first, Buffalo Bill and Nate Salsbury had to work hard to build up their show and profits were poured back into better equipment and new acts. The enterprise was christened 'Buffalo Bill's Wild West – America's National Entertainment'. To underline its authenticity the word 'show' never appeared in its publicity. Salsbury was the vice president and business brain behind the project. Although he was an accomplished actor, singer and comedian he never appeared in the show itself. He remained behind the scenes planning and developing the programme and selecting the cities in which it would appear. All did not run smoothly. The show opened in St Louis in the spring of 1884 and Salsbury, who was still involved in his other theatrical enterprises, paid a visit shortly before the opening to see how things were going. He found Bill drunk surrounded by a group of equally drunk cronies. Salsbury – a teetotaller—was appalled and turned on his heel and left. He later wrote a strong letter to Bill about his behaviour. The response was astonishing and reveals how desperate Bill was for the venture to succeed: 'I solemnly promise you that after this you will never see me under the influence of liquor. I may take two or three drinks to brace up on; that will be all as long as we are partners. I appreciate all you have done. Your judgement and business is good and from this day on I will do my work to the letter. This drinking surely ends today and your pard will be himself and on deck all the time'. Although the show attracted large crowds, profits built slowly with the need to re-invest. At the end of the first year they were showing a loss of $60,000 – well over a million dollars in today's terms. But soon they were making millions; in 1901 their net profits reached a million dollars each – well over twenty million today. The show played to more than 41,000 people on one night in Chicago. But what made some of the acts so exciting also made them dangerous and accidents were inevitable.

Poster advertising Buffalo Bill's first tour

At Hertford in Connecticut Major Frank North was thrown from his horse and trampled. He was in hospital for several months before briefly re-joining the show but left again in early 1885 and died soon afterwards. A steamboat was hired to take the show from one site to another but it sank taking down all the show's wagons, props, guns, equipment along with buffaloes, donkeys and elk. Bill sent a telegram seeking advice to Salsbury who was performing with his theatrical troop in Denver. Salsbury told him to re-equip and open on time at their next engagement New Orleans.

It was here that a new act joined the show. Phoebe Ann Mosey and her husband Frank Butler performed a shooting double act and had been with a circus, but they disliked the life and hearing that the Wild West's sharpshooter Captain Bogardus had decided to quit were looking for an opportunity to join the show. There was no money for the new act but they were given a three-day trial and were so good they were hired minutes after the first performance. Frank decided his wife would be the star and he her assistant – she became world famous as Annie Oakley and they stayed with the show for seventeen years. Annie was tiny, less than five feet tall, she was twenty-five but looked ten years younger but her act was phenomenal. She could break glass balls shot from one of

Annie Oakley: Little Sure Shot

Captain Bogardus's mechanical traps while riding a galloping horse, she trimmed the ash from a lighted cigar held in Frank's lips and shot coins held between his thumb and forefinger.

At their first meeting Buffalo Bill swept off his hat saying: 'They told me about you, Missy. We're glad to have you'. For the rest of her life Annie was known as Little Missy.

She always opened the show; Major Burke explained why: 'It was our first thought, when we planned the show, that so much shooting would cause difficulty, that horses would be frightened and women and children terrified. …. Miss Oakley comes on very early in the performance. She starts very gently, shooting with a pistol. Women and children see a harmless woman out there and do not get worried .

'Gradually she increases the charge in her rifles until at last she shoots with a full charge. Thus by the time the attack on the stagecoach comes, the audience is accustomed to the sound of shooting. In all our history of the Wild West there has never been a horse frightened sufficiently to run away at any of our outdoor performances'.

Before joining the show Annie had appeared at a theatre in St Louis where Chief Sitting Bull, leader of the Sioux at the Battle of the Little Big Horn, was being exhibited to the paying public. Sitting Bull was so impressed with Annie's shooting that he asked to meet her. He called her 'Little Sure Shot' and adopted her into the Sioux tribe as his daughter. This contact was to prove invaluable for the Wild West show, Major Burke had tried to sign Sitting Bull but he had refused – his earlier brush with show business had not been a happy experience and he had been spat at and heckled by the audience. Now Burke was able to show the chief a picture of Annie and assure him that if he joined the show he could see her every day. The strategy worked and Sitting Bull signed a contract on June 6th 1885. He agreed to appear with the show for four months at fifty dollars a week (about $1,200 or just over £900 a week today) not an inconsiderable sum. He got two weeks pay in advance, a bonus of $125 and the sole right to sell his photographs and autographs. In addition five warriors went with him at twenty five dollars a week each, three woman at fifteen dollars a week and a white interpreter who at sixty dollars earned more than Sitting Bull himself.

Sitting Bull and Buffalo Bill in 1885.

It appears the Chief had a natural ability for personal publicity; he took full advantage of his contract to sell photographs and learned to sign his name. The money he didn't send home he seems to have given to young urchins who hung around him as he couldn't understand how there could be so much poverty in the midst of so much wealth.

Sitting Bull was required to do little in the show apart from ride around the arena on his horse dressed in full regalia. Although some spectators thought it patriotic to boo and hiss, he had expected this. He didn't complain and his appearance in the show was a sensation. In Canada, where the Wild West travelled next, there was no animosity over the death of Custer and the crowds were even more enthusiastic. Sitting Bull was greeted as the 'illustrious Indian general and statesman.'

Buffalo Bill has sometimes been accused of exploiting and ill-treating the Indians in his show but there is no evidence to support this. Indeed his view of the Indians was at variance with that generally prevailing at the time. Thousands of souvenir photographs of him and Sitting Bull were sold bearing the message 'Enemies in '76, Friends in '85'. Bill told one reporter on this tour of Canada: 'The defeat of Custer was not a massacre. The Indians were being pursued by skilled fighters with orders to kill. For centuries they had been hounded from the Atlantic to the Pacific and back again. They had their wives and little ones to protect and they were fighting for their existence'.

It was an extraordinarily successful season making the wages paid to Sitting Bull and his band a bargain. The show grossed over a million dollars (nearly twenty four million dollars; eighteen million pounds today) and made a profit of one hundred thousand dollars (nearly two-point-four million dollars; one-point-eight million pounds today).

Sitting Bull spent only one season with Buffalo Bill before returning home. Five years later, in 1890, he was killed after Buffalo

Bill was unsuccessful in a mission that could have saved his life. Trouble had errupted on the Indian reservations: a fanatic who claimed to be a prophet started what were known as 'Ghost Dances' – religious dances which the participants continued until they dropped from exhaustion. It was believed the ceremony would summon a messiah who would lead them to victory in an uprising against the whites. Sitting Bull had nothing to do with the Ghost Dances but rumours persisted that he did. The army thought that if Buffalo Bill could talk to his old friend and other Indian Chiefs the rebellion could be ended. Bill, who was then on tour in Europe, returned home. However, James McLaughlin, the Indian agent in charge of the reservation on which Sitting Bull lived was angry at what he saw as Bill's unwarranted intervention. He sent a telegram to president, Benjamin Harrison, in protest. Half way to Sitting Bull's camp Buffalo Bill was met by troopers with orders to return. McLaughlin had pursuaded the White House to countermand the army's wishes.

An angry Buffalo Bill returned to Europe believing a great opportunity had been missed. His critics dismissed the attempt as a publicity stunt but Bill believed he could have brought peace to the Indian teritories. He also thought he could have saved Sitting Bull's life as a short time later special police employed by the Indian Agent, McLaughlin, arrested Sitting Bull. The chief, who was then fifty nine, surrendered but was shot in the back by police who said he tried to escape. A hundred Indians were arrested and after peace had been restored the army allowed some of them to join Bill's Wild West.

The start of Buffalo Bill's Wild West coincided with a period when the popularity of outdoor shows was at its greatest. In 1885 more than fifty circuses were touring America. Circus had originated in Europe but the American versions were bigger in every respect, they involved horses, trained animals, travelling menageries, freak shows and a track for horse racing. It was a time of great free street parades and two or three shows a day. Famous circus names were at their height: P.T. Barnum, the Sells Brothers and the Ringling Brothers.

Buffalo Bill's Wild West obviously incorporated some elements of the circus but it was very much promoted on its authenticity. Its advertising proclaimed: 'The Romantic West Brought East in Reality. Everything Genuine ... A Year's Visit West in Three Hours. Actual Scenes in the Nation's Progress to Delight'.

Buffalo Bill said it was: 'A true rescript of life on the frontier as I know it to be, and which no fictitious pen can describe'. It was not only the producers of the show who believed it to be a taste of reality. Mark Twain wrote to Bill: 'Down to its smallest details, the show is genuine, cowboys, vaqueros (Mexican cowboys), Indians, stagecoach, costumes and all; it is wholly free from sham and insincerity and the effects it produced upon me by its spectacles were identical with those wrought upon me a long time ago by the same spectacles on the frontier'. Twain urged Bill to take his show to England: 'It is often said on the other side of the water that none of the exhibitions which we send ... are purely and distinctly American. If you will take the Wild West Show over there you can remove that reproach'. In 1886 the Wild West played an extended six-month season on Staten Island, New York. A reporter for the *New York Dispatch* wrote that the 'attendance of visitors to this extraordinary

Mark Twain. He believed Buffalo Bill's show was accurate down to the smallest detail

exhibition of the realism of life on the frontier seems to increase with each day's performances. The grandstands are packed long before the hour of commencement and the throng, elsewhere on the ground is, in its size, a spectacle of crowded humanity worthy of remembrance'.

Among the visitors was rival showman, P.T. Barnum and the inventor, Thomas Edison. The leading English actor, Henry Irving, then appearing on Broadway, took Bill and Salsbury to dinner and urged them to take the show across the Atlantic. At this time a company was being set up to organise an American exhibition in London which would coincide with Queen Victoria's Golden Jubilee and the directors proposed that the Wild West played a six-month season as part of the exhibition and receive a percentage of the gate receipts.

Sir Henry Irving. He urged Buffalo Bill to take his show to England.

As soon as the Wild West had transferred across New York for its indoor 1886/87 winter season at Madison Square Garden, Major Burke was dispatched to London to look at the proposed site for the exhibition at Earl's Court in West London. The American Exhibition was to be built on a large triangular site, owned by three railway companies, and at that time being used as a rubbish tip. The area appeared unprepossessing at first sight, being well away from

London's main theatres and music halls but it had the great advantage of three direct entrances from different railways stations – Earl's Court, West Kensington and West Brompton. As the land was owned by railway companies tickets to the exhibition could be bought at any railway station in the country. Once developed the site proved ideal.

Annie Oakley photographed in 1922 with a gun given to her by Buffalo Bill.

5. The Wild West Arrives in Essex

A few weeks before the Wild West arrived in England the Governor of Nebraska honoured his state's most famous son by commissioning Bill as a colonel in the National Guard. It's thought likely that the idea came from Major Burke who saw the advantage of the title in class-conscious Britain. From then on Buffalo Bill was always billed as 'Colonel Cody' on the Wild West's publicity.

Major Burke and Nate Salsbury underlined the link with Nebraska by chartering a 4,700-ton steamship by that name to transport the show to London. On Thursday March 31st 1887 the company boarded the vessel in New York. There was a cast of 200 including cowboys, Indians, Mexican vaqueros, Annie Oakley, equipment, backstage staff and animals. It was a massive undertaking. The official catalogue of the American Exhibition listed in detail what was transported, it included: seventeen Indian tepees: forty seven camp and dining tents; the original Deadwood stagecoach; three 'Prairie Schooner' wagons; one Band Wagon; 176 horses; twelve mules; nine elk; two deer; eight wild Texas steers ; sixteen Buffaloes; 200 genuine Mexican and Cowboy saddles; 100 Indian saddles not to mention an armoury containing rifles, shotguns, revolvers, Bowie knives and cavalry sabres as well as an assortment of Indian trophies, listed as 'bows and arrows, war bonnets, war shirts, lances, war clubs, shields, scalps &c.'

As the State of Nebraska sailed from New York, 10,000 people and a flotilla of steamboats, tugs and yachts turned out to bid it farewell. Sitting Bull had been given the opportunity to travel and the Bureau of Indian Affairs would have been happy to see him go and be safely out of trouble. But he declined and offered his second in command, Red Shirt, as an alternative. Red Shirt, like many other Indians on the ship, had never left his reservation but Bill had persuaded the authorities to let them go, promising fair wages and equal treatment with the rest of the company. In return the Bureau of Indian Affairs was content to see potential troublemakers removed from their reservations. However, when the moment came to board, the Indians were reluctant to travel – they were certain that as soon as they lost sight of land death awaited them. It took a great deal of persuasion to get them to climb the gang plank. Red Shirt said they believed as soon as the ship set sail they would be struck by a strange disease that would slowly consume their flesh leaving nothing but the skeleton and even this could never find burial. Reluctantly, however, the Indians boarded and the vessel departed. As they left, the company waved their hats and the Indians performed a war dance on the upper deck. Next day, as the ship ploughed through the Atlantic waves, sea-sickness struck many of the passengers and the Indians began to fear that the tales of a mysterious fatal illness were true after all.

Chief Red Shirt – Sitting Bull's second in command.

Bill wrote later that even Red Shirt – the bravest of his people – 'began to feel his flesh to see if it were really diminishing. The seal of hopelessness stamped upon the faces of the Indians aroused my pity and though sick as a cow ... myself, I used my utmost endeavours to cheer them up and relieve their forebodings. But for two days nearly the whole company was too sick for any other active service than feeding the fishes.' The only passengers able to keep their food down were Annie Oakley and her husband, Frank Butler. However, by day three the waves had subsided and most people were feeling better. Bill called the Indians together in the main saloon and gave them a Sunday address along with Red Shirt who was by then fully recovered from his anxiety about the future. All was well until the seventh day at sea when a tremendous storm blew up and the ship had to lay to for a time. The livestock suffered greatly but the journey passed with the death of just one horse.

As the *State of Nebraska* approached the Thames dozens of yachts, barges, tugs and pleasure craft turned out to meet it and welcome the Wild West to England. From one tug the sound of the 'Star Spangled Banner' drifted on the breeze. The show's Cowboy Band immediately responded with a rendition of Yankee Doodle. The tug carried the reception committee headed by Major Burke and Lord Ronald Gower, a director of the American Exhibition. Bill boarded the tug which sailed to Gravesend on the Kent bank of the river where a large crowd had gathered.

He then embarked on a 'Buffalo Bill Special' train and an hour later arrived at Victoria station in London. From there it was a short journey on the new underground railway to Earl's Court where he found a large reception waiting with food and an unlimited supply of alcohol. Later he had his first trip in a horse-drawn Hansom Cab which whisked him to the Hotel Metropole where he spent his first night in London. Early next morning, Bill rushed back to Gravesend to sail into the city with the rest of his company.

Major Burke had asked the press to stay away from Gravesend, feeling the company would not be at their best after the arduous

Atlantic crossing and promised full access once they were established at Earl's Court. However, the *Globe* newspaper could not resist the temptation of a scoop and dispatched its reporter to Gravesend to meet the incoming ship. He found a waterman willing to take him out and after nearly being run down by the *State of Nebraska* as it approached the port, managed to get on board. And so he was able to give English readers their first home-produced view of the Wild West show: 'The living freight on board the *State of Nebraska* is probably as curious and certainly as mixed as was ever sent afloat. There stood the Redskins, mute and immovable. There in dignified silence they stood dressed in paint and blankets. Haughty in mien, graceful in manner, picturesque in dress, the Red Indians of the Wild West show and the "Last of the Mohicans" are one and the same. …. It would be easy to dilate for hours on … these people as seen on board – the men squatting on the deck or playing cards in the smoking cabin; the women leaning against the boiler house for the sake of warmth, some nursing their little ones on their backs, while others wander to and fro smoking cigarettes. … I have not, however, said anything of the white element in the Wild West Show and this is even more remarkable than the red… the American cowboy is an individual of striking manners, good education and elegant appearance and a jolly good fellow to boot… The average cowboy is above average height, well built, compact and handsome.'

It was a short trip from Gravesend to the Albert Dock in the Port of London and Buffalo Bill's first step into Essex. In those days the London boundary was further up river and the Albert Dock was still in Essex. The local population had been alerted to the arrival of the show by a correspondent who wrote in the *Grays and Tilbury Gazette* that the *State of Nebraska* was expected in a few days. Some of his information was wildly inaccurate – he thought there were 900 Indians on board but he was right when he said they were heading for the 'happy hunting grounds' of the American Exhibition. The correspondent had been at the showground recently and, although visitors would be astonished by its magnitude, he thought it would be very incomplete when it was due to open.

Despite the pessimism of the *Grays and Tilbury Gazette*, Buffalo Bill was in optimistic mood as *The State of Nebraska* steamed up river. It was a bright morning and the trip, he wrote later, brought pleasure to all on board. The ship's officers pointed out the sites of historical interest as they steamed past – including Old Tilbury Fort, across the river from Gravesend. Woolwich with its arsenal and gun factories and Greenwich Naval College set in its magnificent park. As they moved slowly up the tideway Buffalo Bill's attention was drawn to the 'huge fleets of sea-going vessels' and the 'forests of masts and spars stretching away seemingly in illimitable perspective'. The endless docks, he wrote, 'spoke of the majesty of commerce and the overflowing glories of what Englishmen only call "The Port of London"'. It was, he said, a magnificent revelation.

A newspaper reporter was on hand to record the scene as the ship was unloaded: 'Out of the holds fore and aft were swung at rapid intervals either bales of cargo, or horse boxes containing buffalo, horses or other livestock. The whirr of the steam winch, the shouts of the men engaged in landing the cargo and the miscellaneous bustle around were exciting enough to the spectators railed off from the wharf'. But perhaps the most unusual and striking scene was presented by the Indians who stood in the sunshine leaning over the rail watching the activity. 'Looking upon the chiefs, braves and squaws', the reporter wrote, 'one could not help recalling the delightful sensations of youth – the first acquaintance with the Last of the Mohicans, the Great Spirit, Firewater, Laughing Water and the dark Huron warrior.' The animals were not so impressive: 'The buffaloes seemed to us in need of pick-me-ups; and the horses had not, to all outward appearance, much buck left in them. A few days' rest, feeding and exercise at Earl's Court will no doubt put them right again, and it is really proof of good management that the voyage had been so successful.'

As Bill surveyed the scene at the Albert Dock he was in a reflective mood: '… as my eyes wandered over the crowded waterway with its myriads of crafts of every description, from the quaint channel fishing-boat to the mammoth East India trader and the ocean steamers, topped by the flags of all nations and hailing from ready accessible part of the known world, carrying the productions of every clime and laden with every commodity, I thought of the magnitude of the enterprise I was engaged in and wondered what its results would be.

'The freight I had brought with me across the broad Atlantic was such a strange and curious one that I naturally wondered whether, after all the trouble, time and expense it had cost me, this pioneer cargo of Nebraska goods would be marketable… A certain feeling of pride came over me when I thought of the good ship on whose deck I stood, and that her cargo consisted of early pioneers and rude, rough riders … wild horses, buffalo, deer, elk and antelope – the king of the game prairie – together with over one hundred representatives of that savage foe that had been compelled to submit to a conquering civilisation and were now accompanying me in friendship, loyalty and peace … all of us combined in an exhibition intended to prove to the centre of the old world civilisation that the vast region of the United States was finally and effectively settled by an English-speaking race.'

Bill's time for reflection was limited – before continuing the journey to Earl's Court everyone had to pass through customs on the Essex shore. This was achieved without a hitch thanks, he wrote, 'to the courtesy of the customs house people.'

6. The American Exhibition

It was a dozen miles from the Albert Dock to Earl's Court and three special trains were diverted from the nearby Gallions station along the wharf to transport the company direct to the exhibition site. The operation went smoothly and Bill reported 'by four o'clock that afternoon the horses were in the stables, watered, fed and bedded, camp equipage and bedding distributed; our own regular camp cooks were hastening a meal; tents were going up, stoves being erected, tables spread and set in the open air; tepees rapidly erected and by six o'clock a perfect canvas city had sprung up in the heart of West-End London.'

The only things missing were the dining tents and the evening meal had to be eaten in full view of what Bill called his 'kindly neighbours'. The meal was finished by seven and by nine the camp was almost complete 'as if it had been there for months and its tired occupants, men, women and children, were reposing more snugly and peacefully than they had done in many weeks.'

Although a large and luxurious tent was erected for Bill, he spent the first weeks of the season comfortably at the Hotel Metropole in Northumberland Avenue. However, he visited the arena early each day to supervise the run up to the opening of the show. Despite his workload, Bill was in demand on the London social scene with invitations flooding in each day. One was to lunch with Oscar Wilde at his house in Chelsea. On a visit to the Reform Club he was introduced to the Prince of Wales who he invited to see the Wild West, little thinking his invitation would be accepted.

Not only was the Prince delighted to accept Bill's invitation but a short time later a message arrived to say he'd like a private performance before the official opening.

So, on the afternoon of Thursday May 5th 1887 a special 'royal rehearsal' version of the show was performed – four days ahead of the opening. The royal party included the Prince and Princess of Wales and their three daughters along with assorted European royalty and lords and ladies in waiting.

The *Era* newspaper described the show, which began with a grand processional review in which all of the Indians, cowboys, scouts, and Mexicans took part: ' After riding round at full gallop, the whole of the band formed a long line and advanced, with Colonel Cody at their head, towards the grandstand. A race between a cowboy, a Mexican, and an Indian, on ponies, followed; after which an illustration was given of an attack by Indians on an emigrant wagon, the frontiersmen eventually driving off their assailants. Then came shooting feats by Miss Oakley and Miss Smith (Lillian Smith was just sixteen and billed as the "Champion California Huntress"), a race between frontier girls, and the riding of bucking horses by cowboys. The exciting incident of the attack on the Deadwood stagecoach by Indians and the rescue by "Buffalo Bill" and his band of scouts followed, and after this a realistic representation of Indian camp life was witnessed. The closing scene was the most exciting of the show. In the centre of the arena stood a settler's cabin, the head of the family having, it was to be presumed, just returned from a hunting expedition, when suddenly a hostile Indian appeared, and was promptly shot by the settler. A band of savages immediately rushed from all directions, and, after a desperate combat, the cabin seemed to be on the eve of capture, when, with a ringing cheer, " Buffalo Bill" and his scouts dashed up and dispersed the Indian braves. At the conclusion the principal performers were presented to the Prince and Princess of Wales. The Indians seemed greatly to appreciate the Royal visit, and "Red Shirt," to whom the Prince was introduced ... said it made his heart glad that one so high above other men should visit him. Though his skin was red and the pale-faced chief's was white, their hearts were one. The Prince then handed Red Shirt a number of cigarettes, which the latter passed round to his companions. A number of relics of Indian fights were shown to the Royal party, including tomahawks, bows and arrows, and scalps. All the Royal visitors expressed themselves highly pleased with the exhibition, and, on leaving, the Prince warmly complimented Colonel Cody and the directors, and expressed the wish that the venture would prove a grand success.'

And great success it was, the show opened in glorious weather on Monday 9th May 1887. *The Times* estimated that 28,000 people passed through the turnstiles that day. Bill wrote later that the moment the doors opened there was a 'great rush of the populace and our money takers had all their work cut out, "with both hands" to relieve the bustling, perspiring crowd of the harmless necessary shillings that flowed in silver streams into our coffers'. While the American Exhibition was felt to be a disappointment, no one was unhappy with Buffalo Bill's Wild West. The show was performed against a vast scenic canvas backdrop depicting the prairie, complete with mountains, rocks and trees. A high rostrum stood to one side of the arena and from there the 'orator', Frank Richmond, introduced proceedings, commented on them and explained western life, traditions and culture. Frank Richmond was possessed of a tremendous voice and the *Daily Telegraph* noted that without the aid of a loudhailer he was audible in all parts of the arena. Tension had mounted as the time for the first performance approached, the crowd stood for the 'Star Spangled Banner' and Frank Richmond launched the show with the words: 'Ladies and Gentlemen, Buffalo Bill and Nate Salsbury proudly present America's National Entertainment, the one and only, genuine and authentic, unique and original ... Wild West'.

The idea that Buffalo Bill's Wild West was very much a reality show was heavily promoted in the American Exhibition's catalogue. 'No exhibition of "America in miniature"', it said, 'would be complete without a faithful representation of the conditions of life in the far West.' The Wild West exhibit was 'designed to illustrate life of the frontiers-man and the North American Indian and to graphically portray the methods by which the United States have been civilised, from Atlantic to Pacific coast. It must be distinctly born in mind that this representation is given by real people, who have been brought five thousand miles from their prairie homes, and by Indians taken from their reservations by permission of the United States Government.'

The exhibition catalogue described the encampment set up near the main arena. This, it said, gave an exact idea of life in the camp of Indian fighters on the one hand and their enemies on the other. The Indian camp consisted of bands of Sioux, Cheyenne, Ogallallas, Arapahoes, Shoshones and other tribes. They were living in their 'high conical tents', known as tepees and decorated with 'rude drawings, symbols of their sign language.' The catalogue said the Indians were 'accompanied by their "squaws" and "papooses" or wives and children'.

The catalogue also provided a vivid picture of the cowboys. The word cowboy, it said, was used to describe the most expert and accomplished herder of cattle. It added: 'A cowboy passes through the various grades of range-worker, cow-puncher, brander, herder, road worker, and trail guide, until he is competent to command a large body of assistants, and safely care for and pilot thousands of heads of cattle ... More than this he is an accomplished Indian fighter and rifle shot, and necessarily a superb horseman.'

The authenticity of Buffalo Bill's show was stressed in a long article in the *Illustrated London News*: 'It is not a circus, nor indeed is it acting at all, in a theatrical sense; but an exact reproduction of daily scenes in frontier life, as experienced and enacted by the very people who now form the "Wild West" Company. It comprises Indian life, "cowboy" life, Indian fighting and burning Indian villages, lassoing and breaking in wild horses, shooting, feats of strength, and Border athletic games and sports. It could only be possible for such a remarkable undertaking to be carried out by a remarkable man: the Hon. W.F. Cody, known as "Buffalo Bill," guide, scout, hunter, trapper ...'

The Times also took up the reality theme: 'As a mere show the display of cowboys, scouts, Indians and horses is exciting and attractive; but it is something more. These men and women are not merely trained circus people; they represent nobody but themselves and their own life in the Wild West. …. Colonel Cody... as scout, soldier, huntsman and rancher has achieved a high reputation all over the States.... Both he and Red Shirt, the mild-looking Sioux chief, have taken many a scalp, and on opposite sides too, though now the latter has evidently resigned himself to the fate of his people, and, like the other Indians, regards Buffalo Bill as his great chief.... Red Shirt is in reality the third chief in rank of the great Sioux Nation, Sitting Bull being the first; at the same time Red Shirt is their greatest fighting man, and was actually among the Indian band of warriors that watched Buffalo Bill's duel with Yellow Hand'.

The show itself was described in the weekly *Reynolds's Newspaper*: 'Within the arena set apart for Buffalo Bill's show, a most picturesque spectacle presented itself. Two-thirds round the expanse set apart for the evolutions of the redskins, the Western cowboys, and their various cavalcades, has been constructed an enormous range of seats, which rise tier above tier. This was absolutely crowded with a dense mass of spectators. On one side may be seen - and the make-believe is most perfect - the blue skies of California, its rocky canons, (sic) and its waving pine-trees. Punctually to the moment appointed,

…. The orator of the show, Mr Frank Richmond, made his appearance in the stand, … and proceeded clearly, in a voice which reached every individual, to describe the various items of the performance … At the far end of the ground, yet apart from the exercises of the Sioux and their *confreres*, a long procession of braves and Indian warriors was now seen making its appearance, gaily garbed in moccasins and feathers, daubed from head to heel in hideous green or yellow ochre, and presenting a fluttering of finery, the chief artistic merit of which was its violent contrast of tint. As the redskins entered the enclosure, and while the long line of riders and steeds was still coming into the field of view, they wheeled sharply round, and the various bands of colour seen as the whole tribe deployed was striking in the extreme.

'The several tribes into which Buffalo Bill's contingent of Indians is divided were then described by the orator as they shot ahead at a hard gallop, and then suddenly checking the speed of their steeds, reined in as immovable as statues, within a few paces of the grand stand. After a race, and such illustrations of frontier life as an old- fashioned pony race, an attack on an emigrant train by the Indians and its defence by frontier's men was depicted. The wagons composing the train, with the emigrants within, and covered with linen, plough their way across the plain, when suddenly, with a wild, savage yell, the Indians appear and dash forward, firing as they speed towards the point of attack, many of them hanging upon the sides of their horses and firing under the neck. The emigrants respond, hurriedly compelling their cattle to lie down, and making temporary breastments of their bodies. The battle is changed in favour of the attacked by the appearance of the frontier's men, who discharge shot after shot with their revolvers with telling effect… After some very clever shooting by Miss Annie Oakley, … and illustrations of " cowboys' fun " in throwing the lariat, and picking up objects from the ground while riding at full speed, the audience were treated to a spectacle of some very clever riding, several members of Buffalo Bill's troupe mounting bucking horses and ponies, which dash about in a manner which threatened to dislocate their own backbones, and much more to injure anyone who dared to try to ride them. In almost every case, however, the cowboys were successful in mastering their steeds.

'More ride shooting by Miss Lilian Smith, and horseback riding by American frontier girls, led up to the attack on the Deadwood stagecoach by Indians, and their repulse by cowboys commanded by Buffalo Bill... The Deadwood coach, with its solid india-rubber springs and ancient woodwork, was drawn rapidly along the ring by its team of mules. Suddenly the Indians appear on the horizon, and with a wild war-whoop bear down upon it. The passengers in the coach respond vigorously with their revolvers, and in the end Buffalo Bill and his followers give a good account of themselves, and the Indians are obliged to sheer off... A race between Sioux Indian boys on bare-backed Indian ponies, and another between Mexican thoroughbreds, were followed by an illustration of the phases of Indian life. As the nomadic tribes were seen camped on the prairie, an attack by hostile Indians was made, and this was followed by a scalp, war, and other dances... Buffalo Bill, "America's practical all-round shot," then gave an exhibition of roping and riding of wild Texas steeds by cowboys and Mexicans... After an illustration of the buffalo hunt came an attack upon a settler's cabin by hostile redskins, which was vivid to a degree.'

Despite some criticism of the treatment of animals in parts of the show, the opening was a triumph and other papers were lavish in their praise.

The *Daily Telegraph* wrote: 'Buffalo Bill, mounted on a beautiful white horse, and looking a veritable ' king of men', as fine a figure as he is an admirable and elegant horseman. No sight-seer has ever beheld before a picture so varied and brilliant'.

The *Standard* wrote of 'A host of curious illustrations of American ingenuity.'

The *Morning Post* noted: ' The performance was received with the utmost enthusiasm throughout.'

The *Daily News* called it: 'A very bright and pretty show. "A magnificent collect of heads, horns and bodies of beasts of the chase." ... So many people in such serried array were never before seen under one roof in this country.'

The *Sportsman* predicted 'The Wild West Show will be London's most popular attraction during the Jubilee Year.'

The *Illustrated Sporting* and *Dramatic News* devoted a whole page to the show as did the *Pall Mall Gazette* which also linked Buffalo Bill to Queen Victoria's Golden Jubilee and noted the events were 'the two great booms of the year 1887' (see pages 58/59).

Just two days after the opening the Queen herself decided to see what all the fuss was about. The Prince of Wales had obviously given his mother an enthusiastic account of his visit and an official document was delivered to Earl's Court saying that Her Majesty 'by royal command' requested a private performance. It was to last no longer than one hour and be attended by the Queen and a few members of the royal household. It was an amazing coup for Buffalo Bill – it would be the first time the Queen had attended a performance in a public venue since the death of Prince Albert twenty six years earlier.

The Royal Command proved difficult and expensive – it meant cancelling a public show that would have been seen by up to 40,000 people on only the second day of its run. The show also had to be cut to less than an hour.

The Royal Box built for the visit of the Prince and Princess of Wales just days earlier was quickly re-built with a dais at the centre on which the Queen was seated. Bill wrote later that the box was draped with crimson velvet and decorated with orchids, leaving plenty of room for the 'attendant notables'. With the preparations complete he and the rest of the cast waited like a 'lot of schoolboys attending an examination.'

The show went well, at one stage the American flag was carried around the arena on horseback and Buffalo Bill later claimed the Queen and the royal party had risen from their seats and bowed. It was, he said, a great event: 'For the first time in history, since the Declaration of Independence, a sovereign of Great Britain had saluted the star-spangled banner, and that banner was carried by a member of Buffalo Bill's Wild West…. We felt the hatchet had been buried at last and Wild West had been at the funeral.'

After the show, Bill was presented to the Queen. She was, he wrote: 'A kindly little lady, not five feet in height, but every inch the gracious queen'. What she said to Bill remains unrecorded. He wrote later: 'Her compliments, deliberate and unmeasured, modesty forbids me to repeat'.

The Queen, however, did record her thoughts in her diary. That night she wrote: 'All the different people, wild, painted Red Indians from America, on their wild bare backed horses, of different tribes – cow boys, Mexicans, &c, all came tearing round at full speed, shrieking and screaming, which had the weirdest effect. An attack on a coach & on a ranch, with an immense deal of firing, was most exciting, so was the buffalo hunt, & the bucking ponies…that were almost impossible to sit. The cowboys are fine looking people…but the painted Indians, with their feathers, & wild dress (very little of it) were rather alarming looking, and they have cruel faces. …Col. Cody 'Buffalo Bill', as he is called… is a splendid man, handsome & gentlemanlike in manner.'

THE AMERICAN EXHIBITION AND WILD WEST SHOW.

The American Exhibition at Earl's Court was opened yesterday with considerable éclat. There was the luncheon usual on such occasions, and the speeches were printed and circulated like handbills to counteract, of course, any defect in the acoustic defects of the building. The Director-General gave a florid address, and Lord Ronald Gower did duty for "our noble selves." The exhibition itself is not in a very forward state, but no doubt a few weeks will make many changes for the better. But the chief exhibit at the American Exhibition is Mr. Cody's Circus, or, as it is called, the Wild West Show, which has excited popular imagination for some weeks past, partly by adroit advertisement and partly by flamboyant posters. Indeed, "Buffalo Bill" and the Jubilee are the two great booms of the year 1887. Mr. Irving, the tragedian, and Mr. Partington, the bill-poster, have each contributed to make Mr. Cody, alias "Buffalo Bill," the most talked about man in London. The "braves" and the "squaws" have been taken to church, much to the edification of the congregation, who found them much more entertaining than the service, and more attractive than a gorgeous ritual. The other day the Prince of Wales inspected the show. It is a mere commonplace to remark that the Prince of Wales has also become a useful advertising medium in this year of grace. Only the Archbishop of Canterbury and General Booth are left, and they will probably be drawn into the advertising vortex. So the merry game of advertising has been pursued. Has not the Princess of Wales patted the hideous little papooses on the head, and the Prince doled out cigarettes to the "redskins"? Has not Mr. Gladstone conferred with Red Shirt in his wigwam? and has not Miss Terry experienced a new emotion? Is it surprising, then, that at

BUFFALO BILL.

THE SQUAWS AT HOME.

THE CAMP AT EARL'S COURT.

"DOING THE DOLCE" AND A CIGARETTE.

to represent sky, mountain, and rolling prairies. From two till four the crowd crushed in and took their places till not a seat was vacant, and there must have been at least 10,000 people present, including, one would say, the whole of the theatrical profession. Mr. Irving led in Miss Ellen Terry (the Royalties of the profession), exacting a sort of universal homage from the assembled multitude of fashionables. We are not going to enumerate them, leaving that duty to the *World*, which has recently become a sort of fashionable directory. Nor, indeed, is there much need to describe at any length the performance of Buffalo Bill and his men. Among the company is a gentleman called the "orator," who takes up a position on a timber structure, and from there directs the manoeuvres, and gives a sort of running commentary on them like a glorified bellman. We may at once say that the circus justifies its reputation. The camp, the redskins, the prowess of Buffalo Bill and Buck Taylor, the riding of the cowboys, the shooting of the ladies, the sticking up of the Deadwood Coach, the war dance, the bloodthirsty attack on the little log hut in the centre of the arena—have they not been described at length in every paper in Great Britain and America? There are some wonderful feats of riding and shooting. The buck jumpers excited extraordinary interest, for such a display of horsemanship has never been seen here before. To see Buck Taylor pick up a handkerchief from the ground going full tilt on a fiery mustang is worth a long journey to see. Buffalo Bill does very little himself besides taking a few turns on his grey horse, firing at glass balls on horseback, and cracking a bullock whip. Only one portion of the entertainment failed to please the audience, and that was the bull-baiting by a crowd of vacqueros, who lashed the poor beast with ropes, to illustrate the use of the lassoo. This was roundly hissed, and should be stopped at once, unless they wish for the interference of the Society for the Prevention of Cruelty to Animals. We want no bull-baiting here, and Mr. Nate Salsbury must be told so pretty sharply. Those who wish to know more of Buffalo Bill's career must be referred to the highly-coloured book which is sold in the grounds. Bill Cody is a famous scout, who has seen much hard fighting in his day. He earned his sobriquet of "Buffalo Bill" by supplying meat to the men who were building the Pacific Railway, and is said to have killed for them nearly five thousand buffaloes. He is a good shot, a good horseman, and a handsome fellow. But Mr. Partington's portraits are very faithful representations of the wild man of the West. In the course of time the railway was done, the navvies moved on, and there was no longer any necessity for butcher's meat; the Red Man, degenerated by fire-water and tobacco, died out, and Buffalo Bill began to look around him for a new job. So the story goes. The result is the present show. As for the Indians, why they are the most picturesque fellows ever seen. Our sketches may give some idea of their camp at Earl's Court.

A MYSTERY MAN.

least 10,000 people, most of them guests, it is true, passed through the turnstiles to see the first performance? Mr. Cody should feel highly delighted with the result, which we are bound to say in most respects justifies Mr. Irving's recommendation and Mr. Partington's posters. During the ceremony in the exhibition proper the crowds flocked into the seats which run half round the circle formed by the arena. The other half is hung with canvas painted

Both the Pall Mall Gazette and the Illustrated Sporting and Dramatic

OUR CAPTIOUS CRITIC.

BUFFALO BILL'S WILD WEST.

Land of the West, fair land of the Wild West Brompton, I salute thee. Land of the Star - spangled Banner (*Vexillum stellatum*), and the bald - headed Eagle (*Aquila calva*), of the Big Boom (*Malus ingens*) and the Almighty Dollar (*Obolus omnipotens*); land of Buffalo Bill (*Bubalus sympraphus*) and Buck Taylor (*Cervus savior*) of Annie Oakley (*Anas querula*) and Lilian Smith (*Faber illiscens*), sweet it is in thee to renew the delights of my childhood, to stand face to face with the noble red - man and the heroes of Beadle's American Library.

I tread the halls of the American Exhibition, and I hail the true Republican boldness which seeks to elevate a trading bazaar to the dignity of a national institution. I mark the swarming dead-head (*Caput mortuum*), and note the transatlantic adaptability with which each official assumes the part of the big chief (*Primus infatus*) when addressed by him.

I wander further afield into the Wild West itself. I enter the camp. I see the Indian seated stoically at the entrance of his wigwam dreaming of the happy hunting grounds, and chasing in thought the nimble green-back (*Tergum viride*). I watch the cowboy (*Vaccious puer*) engaged in the consumption of the cheering cocktail (*Cauda galli*). I hear with awe the words of wisdom addressed by Red Shirt (*Indusius rubricatum*) to the grand old Orator (*Loquisimus garrulosus*).

I am back in the secretary's office. I see a figure seated in one corner in the attitude of a limp Guy Fawkes. On its head is a broad-brimmed sombrero; round its waist is a belt with a huge diamond buckle; on its legs are buckskin gaiters, and on its feet—strange contrast—boots of patent leather. It sits limp, silent, and melancholy, in the attitude of Grandfather Smallweed. Only for a time. For lo! the word is given and Buffalo Bill starts up to his full height, and sallies out with the majesty of Republican manhood to receive the Prince and Princess of Wales.

The opening ceremony! I see the executive, with a noble disregard of the whole practices of an Old World monarchy, repudiating the patronage of the official representative of their country. I listen to the strange blending of orations, prayers, and the strains of "The Star-Spangled Banner." I see the enthusiastic charge of the wild free-lumber. I note the con-

tinued clash of conflicting orders, and the consequent jam of struggling humanity. And I sigh for the presence of a sufficiency of the A division of police, who at least have the merit of knowing how to put the right people in the right place.

The show. The "orator" mounts a scaffold near the centre of the arena. He announces that the performance of the Wild West is unrehearsed. The performers enter, and bear out his statement. Another noble instance of a refusal to don the social shackles of a worn out continent.

The grand processional review of the Wild West sweeps by at the word of command. The prairie schooners lumber across the plain, and the attack upon them of the Indians is repulsed by the frontiersman. The cowboys mount the bucking pony and cast the lariat. The Virginia reel is danced on horseback. No base imitation this of the quadrille gone through in the stereotyped circuses of the Old World, but the free wild outcome of Western enthusiasm. The tame buffalo waddles placidly into the enclosure, and is spurred to a gentle trot by having his hind-quarters singed with blank cartridge. The equally tame Texas steer is roped and jerked off his legs in a wholly unnecessary and uncalled for fashion. The Indian brave dances the war dance of his tribe in full war paint, and very little else. The Deadwood Stage Coach comes rattling up drawn by its team of six. The same number of unsuspecting passengers are induced to enter it. It rattles off on its journey across the plain. Again the Indians swoop down to the attack. Again, like a member of the Salvation Army, it receives its "baptism of blood and fire." Again the heroic cowboys dash to the rescue. Again savage and Saxon mingle fiercely in mimic conflict. Again the Indian retires before the irresistible onslaught of Western manhood.

I see the Wild Huntress of the Plains step forward. She lifts the deadly shooting iron. She levels it with unerring aim against the glass ball (*Globus vitreus*) and the clay pigeon (*Columba argillacea*). She hits her mark—when she does not miss it. But her hands are not imbued with the blood of the innocent down, as are those of the ruthless aristocrats of the European gun clubs.

The Indian attack. The settler's cabin stands out on the broad Bromptonian plain. The wily Indian lurks hard by amidst the canvas cliffs bounding its far-stretching expanse. He lurks very visibly. The settler's wife prepares for the evening meal by nearly setting the chimney on fire. The settler's brother rides up with a deer on his saddle-bow. He makes signs to the settler that it must be cooked at once. The settler points to his stock of firewood, and explains that this is impossible. The brother, in a rage, takes it out of his horse by savagely

News devoted whole pages to the opening of the Wild West at Earl's Court

The Wild West gave 300 performances during the 1887 Earl's Court season ending on October 31st. The weather that summer had been glorious and two-and-a-half million people saw the show – more than half the population of London.

Buffalo Bill himself had missed not a single performance and now set out to conquer the provinces. He moved first to Birmingham before heading to Manchester for the winter where the show would play for five months in a new, purpose built, steam-heated stadium. Annie Oakley and her husband left the show after the London season and her place on the bill was taken by Johnny Baker, The Cowboy Kid, who had first met Bill when he was nine years old. He was now an accomplished marksman. After the winter in Manchester the Wild West returned in triumph to New York where it played the summer season on Staten Island before moving on to Philadelphia, Washington Baltimore and Richmond.

A group of Buffalo Bill's Wild West Indians

7. Across the Atlantic Again

In 1890 the show again set sail for Europe, Annie Oakley returned and would stay for the next ten years. The European tour included a seven-month season in Paris followed by visits to Spain, Italy, Austria and Germany.

In 1891 the show returned to Britain, this time with twenty three Indian prisoners of war who had been released to Buffalo Bill's care after the 'ghost shirt' uprising and the death of Sitting Bull. The season opened in Leeds in June followed by one or two week seasons around the country in cities including Liverpool, Manchester, Sheffield Cardiff, Portsmouth and Glasgow. There was another Earl's Court season from May to July 1892 and another command for a private performance from Queen Victoria – this time at Windsor. By that time a party of Cossack horsemen had joined the show and during their performance the Queen's son-in-law, Prince Henry of Battenburg, asked her in German whether she thought they were genuine Cossacks. Nate Salsbury, who spoke the language fluently, was quick to assure them that the show still remained firmly rooted in reality, telling the Queen: 'I beg to assure you ... that everything and everybody you see in the entertainment are exactly what we represent them to be'.

The show travelled back to Essex – this time to Tilbury docks – for its departure to New York on the American steamship *Mohawk*. The vessel left on October 14th 1892 and it was to be ten years before the Wild West returned to England.

Although the emphasis of the show was still on reality, the addition of the 'Cossacks of the Caucasus' in 1892 and later other foreign participants such as French Chasseurs and British and German Lancers marked the start of something much more varied. The name of the show was changed to ' Buffalo Bill's Wild West and Congress of Rough Riders of the World.' The term Rough Rider was used by Bill several years before it was adopted by Theodore Roosevelt, then a Lieutenant Colonel and later US President, for his cavalry forces after they defeated the Spanish in Cuba at the the battle of San Juan Hill during the Spanish-American War. A recreation of this battle later featured in the Wild West show.

As the show grew so did the expenses and it started losing money. It was costing $4,000 a day to run (more than $90,000 – £70,000 today). To make matters worse, by the end of the 1894 season Nate Salsbury had been taken ill with a stomach complaint and was unable to take part in the day-to-day management of the show.

In 1895 he came to an agreement with James M. Bailey of the Barnum and Bailey circus empire who would provide transportation for the show and cover local expenses for a share of the profits. To rescue the Wild West from debt Bailey used the circus idea of one-day engagements at towns across the country. While the Barnum and Bailey Circus was away touring Europe, he used his circus railway cars to move the Wild West around America. It covered 9,000 miles and visited 131 cities in 190 days. Although Buffalo Bill, who was now in his fifties, found the pace exhausting the tour was a financial success.

The arrival of Bailey, although the arena Wild West performance remained the centre of the show, saw the introduction of many sideshows. These included a boy giant, a midget, a sword swallower, fire eater and even Venetian glassblowers. The arena show itself was expanded to include items which had little to do with the western theme. The key idea of reality remained, however, and topical items introduced to the show included scenes from the Spanish-American War and the Boxer rebellion in China. In addition to the Cossacks, British Lancers, Arabs, gauchos from Argentina and Japanese mounted Samurai were also included in the show.

Whenever he could Bill returned to his home in Wyoming. In the mid 1880s he had been instrumental in the creation of the town of

Cody, in the north west of the state, which still bears his name today. He had first passed through the region in the 1870s and was impressed with the development possibilities of the rich soil, grand scenery and proximity to Yellowstone Park. He established the TE Ranch about thirty five miles from Cody on a fork of the Shoshone River. It boasted a spacious ranch house where he often entertained important guests from Europe and America and remained his home for the rest of his life.

In 1902 The Wild West was ready to cross the Atlantic once again. Before leaving, Nate Salsbury returned for a final time to oversee the introduction of items new to the British audience. These included the Battle of San Juan Hill, which featured some of the men who had actually taken part in the war under the command of Teddy Roosevelt and a display by US life guards. Salsbury was by this time too weak to shout and sat in a chair while Johnny Baker – The Cowboy Kid – relayed his directions. The show set sail from New York at the beginning of December 1902 for a season at Olympia in London before touring the country. By the end of October 1903 it had travelled nearly 3,000 miles and performed in almost one hundred towns and cities.

Despite the changes, newspapers stressed the show was still based in reality. The *Sporting Life* wrote: 'It is worthy of note that all the people who take part in the "Buffalo Bill" exhibition are genuinely what they represent, and not actors and performers trained to impersonate them.

'All of the cowboys have actually spent their lives upon the western plains, while the Indians have been secured by special permission from the United States Government to whom Colonel Cody has become personally responsible for their care and comfort during their stay on this side and their safe return to the reservations at the conclusion of this exhibition.

Newspaper advertisement for the first show of the 1902-03 tour

'The Mexicans are the best representatives of the "ruralities" of that country, the United States Cavalry have all seen active service in the regular army, the Canadian contingent of the mounted police are all picked men from His Majesty's service in the northern forests of the western continent, the United States Life Saving Corps have actually taken part in the rescue of many vessels along the stormy Atlantic coast, the Gauchos are among the hardiest representatives of the Latin races who have made a success of the South American continent, the Cossacks are from His Imperial Russian Majesty's army, while the British cavalrymen who take part in the exhibition have followed the colours at Mafeking and in India. The American Rough Riders have been selected from those who accompanied President (then Colonel) Roosevelt in the dashing charges made during the late war in Cuba.'

Unlike the earlier Earl's Court seasons, the Olympia show was indoors. The show occupied the massive centrally-heated Grand Hall which covered four acres. The first performance was scheduled for Boxing Day 1902.

With Nate Salsbury too ill to travel, Johnny Baker had taken over his role and was credited as 'Arenic Director'. In addition he dropped the name 'The Cowboy Kid' and was billed as 'the celebrated young American marksman' when he appeared in the show.

The first performance of the fourteen week Olympia season was about to start when a telegram arrived addressed to Buffalo Bill himself. It carried the devastating news that Nate Salsbury – Bill's business partner for fourteen years – was dead. Bill wanted to cancel the show but was persuaded to go ahead. The many flags around Olympia were lowered to half-mast and the Stars and Stripes carried around the arena at the start of the show was draped in black crepe. As the show opened Bill rode to the head of the assembled company, approached the Royal Box – occupied by among others the Duke and

Duchess of Argyll – and announced 'Ladies and Gentlemen permit me to introduce to you a congress of rough riders of the world'. The show was a resounding success. The *Observer's* correspondent wrote: 'The show is great in every way – in size, in variety, in interest, even in instruction. It provides an alluring picture of life in (the) Wild West …. It presents a picture of life under exciting conditions in a country all have read about and many have seen. Marvellous things are here — the actual things, horsemanship feats of great wonder, life on the plains, life under conditions altogether strange and fascinating. … An Indian camp and a horse show are special features of an entertainment where all is special and noteworthy. Colonel Cody is most popular in this country. His show is bigger and brighter than ever before. He has received the heartiest welcome. To this fascinating Wild West show everyone, young folks and old, should go. Nowhere else can anything like it be seen.'

The show was notable in one other minor respect – the Deadwood stagecoach that now found itself pursued around the arena was no longer the original. That had become worn out and was given to the Smithsonian Institution in Washingon. It can still be seen today at the Buffalo Bill Historical Centre, an affiliate of the Smithsonian in Wyoming.

There were many visits to the show by minor royalty but it was not until the middle of March that King Edward VII and Queen Alexandra attended a performance. The King was keen to re-acquaint himself with the show which he had enthusiatically supported when it first opened in London in 1887. In addition to the Queen, he was accompanied by other members of the royal family including his grandson who was to become Duke of Windsor and briefly King Edward VIII. By the end of the season in early April audiences were dwindling but, undaunted, Bill set off for the summer tour.

8. On the Road

After the Olympia run, the show moved to Manchester for three-weeks and then to Liverpool for a similar period but with the exception of two weeks in Birmingham and a week in Cardiff it was mainly one-day appearances. Moving the Wild West show was a massive task carried out with military precision. Everything, which in addition to the cast – human and animal – included the arena with covered seating for more than 12,000 people, scenery and an electric lighting plant, had to be loaded onto the three trains provided by Barnum and Bailey. In total there were some fifty carriages of which eight carried the staff and performers.

Sleeping arrangements were far from luxurious for the standard workers. There were slatted wooden bunks, four high on each side of a narrow walkway accommodating around seventy people per coach. There were no cooking facitities and just one toilet at each end of the carriage. The private car used by Buffalo Bill was a little more luxurious with a bedroom, living room and office. In addition there were carriages for the animals and flat bed cars for the equipment. Two of the trains were more than 350 yards long and the third 300 yards.

The job of supervising this vast transport undertaking fell to Fred Hutchinson who was James Bailey's nephew. As they moved from town to town he oversaw the unloading of the trains, the moving of the 800 staff and performers plus scores of animals to the show site where a tented city was created and the arena assembled. Two shows were presented before the whole operation was reversed; as the last act was unfolding in the arena everything not needed was being dismantled ready to move on. When the show arrived at its destination the unloading of equipment began immediately. The operation followed a strict pattern – first everything needed to transform the showground into a small town was put on wagons pulled by teams of draught horses.

The Sphere *newspaper marked the opening of the Wild West's 1902-03 tour with a full front-page picture*

These carried tons of canvas, ropes, stakes and other equipment. Most sites were on the outskirts of town as the show required an area of some eleven acres. Although performed in the open air, the audience was sheltered by a three-sided covered grandstand consisting of two long sides of 320 feet and a short side of 150 feet. The other short side was the backdrop and the entrance point for performers. In addition to the main arena there were accommodation and dining tents, sideshow and souvenir stalls and pens for the buffalo, horses and other livestock. Most of the canvas structures could be erected within two hours. Among the largest of these were the backdrops and while not as detailed as those used during extended engagements they were still impressive with each scene requiring 300 lbs of paint. Usually there were two scenes one behind the other which could be drawn back to allow the entry of performers.

Buffalo Bill had his own tent, well furnished with carpets, easy chairs and photographs and here he would often entertain distinguished visitors. The show also had a number of road vehicles carrying everything from canvas to confectionery and these were painted in yellow livery.

Some of the wagons needed to haul equipment from the railway to the showground were thirty five feet long and required a team of eight horses to pull them. The electric lighting equipment was a novelty in its own right and in towns where there were street parades it was drawn through the streets by a six-horse team. The vehicle had a large brass boiler along with flywheels and other machinery. It was a massive contraption with rear wheels six feet high. The scale of catering required for this huge enterprise was itself astonishing. Around the time the show visited Essex the 800 people travelling with it were said to be consuming 1,400 lbs of meat daily as well as seven hundredweight of potatoes, 450 lbs of bread and thirty hundredweight of miscellaneous vegetables. All in all 2,100 meals were served daily requiring ten cooks and sixty waiters.

Another vast undertaking was the amount of publicity which had to be generated to ensure the paying public continued to flock to the show. As Buffalo Bill approached Essex for the first time a reporter for the *East Anglian Daily Times* was dispatched to uncover the facts. 'The general public', he wrote, 'has little idea of the amount of detail and labour involved in advertising an exhibition of the character and magnitude of Buffalo Bill's Wild West.' A team of some forty five people journeyed exactly twenty one days ahead of the show in their own special railway car. In addition to an office, the car also had sleeping quarters as travelling was done at night, workspace, benches and cupboards. Each morning a manager issued instructions and teams were dispatched whose job it was to secure prominent hoardings along railway lines in a fifty mile circumference around the showground and cover them in posters. Another batch of men known as 'country bill-posters' used wagons which had been arranged in advance and which arrived at daybreak to travel local roads in every direction for some twenty miles to stick posters on barns, fences and any other suitable surface. Another set of gangs known as 'city bill-posters' covered hoardings within the town limits and persuaded shopkeepers to display advertising in their shops. Still others went from door to door distributing illustrated leaflets. It was hard work for the men involved. The advertising car carried a large boiler which was used to manufacture the paste required to attach the posters. The men had to get up a four o'clock every morning to make the paste they would need that day. After that they had breakfast before setting out on the real day's work – rain or shine – posting between 13,000 and 20,000 sheets of paper. In all the show visited around ninety English and Welsh towns and cities on the 1903 tour, travelling nearly 3,000 miles by train plus another 270 miles from railway sidings to the showgrounds and back again. Among those ninety stops were three in Essex.

9. Three Days in September – Leyton, Southend and Colchester

The 1903 show consisted of around twenty scenes and lasted some two hours. It began with the American national anthem, 'The Star Spangled Banner', performed by the Cowboy Band. This was followed by the mounted Grand Revue in which all those taking part paraded around the arena before Buffalo Bill galloped in to rousing cheers. Then came an exhibition of riding skills by a cowboy, a Cossack, a Mexican, an Arab, a gaucho and an Indian. Veterans of the 5th US Artillery gave a display of artillery drill using muzzle-loading guns.

A prairie immigrant wagon train was attacked by Indians who were in turn driven off by a group of cowboys. Buffalo Bill thrilled the crowd by shooting glass balls from horseback as they were thrown up by an accompanying cowboy while they galloped around the arena. Johnny Baker also gave a display of sharpshooting often from unusual stances such as laying on his back or shooting through his legs.

Whirling Hawk, a Sioux Indian who appeared with Buffalo Bill

A Pony Express rider gave a demonstration of how letters were carried at high speed across America for a brief period before the coming of the railway and telegraph. A crew from the United States Life Saving Corps demonstrated the use of the mortar in throwing a lifeline and the rescue of those shipwrecked with a breeches buoy.

An impressive view of the 1903 show which visited Leyton, Southend an

Colchester. From the Illustrated Sporting and Dramatic News

Two Wild West show posters. Thousands of posters and leaflets were distributed by the advance publicity team

Veteran American and English cavalrymen carried out military exercises; a group of cowgirls raced on horseback and cowboys rode bucking broncos. Mexicans demonstrated their skill with the lasso; Indians performed war dances; the Battle of San Juan Hill was depicted by soldiers who had actually been there, although some of the Spanish soldiers were played by Indians and Buffalo Bill took the part of Teddy Roosevelt. The Deadwood stagecoach was attacked by Indians before being rescued by cowboys. Finally, a settler's cabin came under siege by Indians who were once again driven off – this time by a group of cowboys led by Buffalo Bill himself. The show ended with a salute from Bill and the entire cast.

One of the star performers was Chief Iron Tail who was a close friend of Bill and a celebrity in his own right. He was later one of three models used to create the Indian Head nickel coin which circulated in America from 1913 to 1938. In the following year's show he was one of two chiefs who led the attack on Custer during the recreation of the Battle of the Little Big Horn. He also oversaw a performance of the ghost dance while on horseback. One reporter described him as 'a dignified warrior and not one to extend friendship too easily'.

The Wild West arrived in Leyton on Wednesday 2nd September 1903. Cast and equipment were ferried from Temple Mills rail yard near Stratford where the special trains had stopped. The showground was on the Barclay Estate which was bounded by Lea Bridge Road, Leyton Green Road and James Lane and was, as one local paper noted, convenient for people travelling from both Leyton and Walthamstow. As usual the show had received maximum publicity from the advance crew and the advertisements proclaimed the reality of what was on show (see page 77). One promised: 'A Veritable Kindergarten of History Teaching Facts'. The show, it said, was 'Taken from the pages of realism and illustrated by the very men who have assisted in making familiar the most famed of the World's Mounted Warriors. A gathering of extraordinary consequence to fittingly illustrate all that has and can be endured by Virile Martial Manhood.'

The show's arrival prompted huge excitement. The *Leyton and District Times* said the evening performance saw 'probably the largest audience ever gathered at a single entertainment in Leyton.' Attendance at the afternoon performance was good, although probably reduced by the rain that came on an hour before it was due to start. In the evening, though, almost every one of the 14,000 seats was occupied.'

The *Leyton and District Times* reporter was ecstatic in his praise: '... such horsemanship as was witnessed in his (Buffalo Bill's) arena on Wednesday has never been seen in Leyton before, and will, in all probability never be seen again. Painted, feather-decked, whooping Indians, bronco riding cowboys. Picturesque Mexicans (and) gauchos conjured up vivid pictures from the half-forgotten pages of Fenimore Cooper and Mayne Reid.' (Thomas Mayne Reid, now long forgotten, was a Scots-Irish American novelist whose stories of the American wild west captivated children around the world). The reporter concluded: 'The marvelous equestrian feats of the Cossacks, the wonderful dexterity of the cowboys in the use of the lasso, the extraordinary accuracy of Buffalo Bill and Johnny Baker's rifle fire, all assisted to make the ... entertainment full of instruction and enthralling interest.'

The *Walthamstow Guardian* newspaper was impressed by the bearing of Buffalo Bill himself. 'A striking figure', it noted, 'is that of the adventurous and intrepid Colonel, and it is easy to understand the influence he exercises over men of varied types and nationalities.' The performance, it went on, 'was full of interest from the beginning to end' and 'the utmost was done to give realism to the scenes illustrative of life on the Western Plains in days gone by.'

Poster advertising the 1903 show

After the main show the evening ended with a concert by a number of singers, dancers, and comedians. The arena had been virtually dismantled before everyone had left. First to go was the generator wagon. By 11.15pm, just over an hour after the performance finished, only the dressing tent remained. Wagons waited for horses to return for a second and third journey to the special trains. The last wagon left at 11.45pm and nothing remained but a mass of paper and other rubbish. This was cleared by a local contractor the following morning. The trains carrying performers and equipment set off for Southend about 2am.

Chief Iron Tail was a star performer when the Wild West came to Essex in 1903 and 1904. He was a close friend of Buffalo Bill and travelled with the show from 1889 until it closed in 1913. He died from influenza in Chicago in 1916.

Two hours later the Wild West rolled into Southend Railway Station (now Southend Victoria) and the horse-drawn wagons immediately set out for the showground at Marine Park. The eighty strong catering team was always first to leave the train when it arrived at a new stop. The fourteen feet long four-wheeled wood and coal-fired catering stove was rapidly sent on its way and by 6am a hot breakfast was ready for the entire company in the massive dining tent.

When a reporter from the *Essex Chronicle* arrived at 10am he was able to confirm that everything was in perfect order and looked as if it had been standing for a month instead of a few hours.

Major John Burke, Buffalo Bill's long-time partner, had gone ahead to ensure maximum newspaper publicity and was rewarded with an article previewing the show in the *Southend Standard*. In it Burke was, as ever, keen to stress the realistic nature of the production. Buffalo Bill, he told the paper, could well feel proud of the 'educative merit' of his exhibition. The show placed the actual people in a way that represented historical incidents and spelled out lessons in the opening and development of America that would otherwise be forgotten. Major Burke said the show taught spectators many things, among them horsemanship and the value of fearlessness in handling a horse so that the animal would recognise man as its master; the art of war and the value of health as promoted by honest exercise. He pointed out that earlier in the year the show had been seen by the King and Queen at Olympia and indeed Queen Alexandra had visited twice within four days.

The show caused huge interest in Southend with cowboys and Indians wandering the streets ahead of the first performance at 2pm. The grounds opened at 11am and visitors were able to look at the Indian tepees and view their inhabitants who were walking around the grounds in their native dress. The *Southend Standard* reported that the ticket office was besieged. This was a wagon painted deep yellow with large decorated wheels and hatches for selling tickets. Admission prices ranged from one shilling (around five pounds today) to seven shillings and six pence – more than thirty five pounds today – so it wasn't a cheap entertainment; the average weekly wage for a farm labourer at the time was around fifteen shillings – about seventy five pounds today.

Before the main arena opened the sideshows did good business, entrance to these was sixpence. Especially popular were

the 'living curiosities'. Among these were the Egyptian giant and the world's smallest midget. The giant claimed to be eight feet two inches and he was seated next to two-feet tall Princess Hawa.

Other attractions included Octavia, a young lady snake charmer, said to be pretty enough to charm anything; Professor Giovanni and his performing cockatoos; a sword swallower and Chinese acrobats.

Another of the sideshows featured the Missouri-born Charles Eldridge Griffin who had joined the Wild West that year. He was a remarkable character who was an author, comedian, conjuror, contortionist, dancer, fire-eater, hypnotist, illusionist, sword swallower, circus manager, newspaper owner and publisher. During this season he performed his 'Yankee Magic'.

Left: Southend Standard advertisement for the show

Griffin stayed with the show for four years and his talents were soon recognized; in 1904 he became the Wild West's manager. He later wrote a book about his experiences and noted that the 1903 season was 'very pleasant and prosperous ... notwithstanding the fact that the elements were against us most of the time...The weather conditions ... were most depressing...'

The afternoon performance began at 2pm and the evening at 8pm. As the audience took their seats, the Cowboy Band played a selection of tunes. The musicians were seated on the band wagon which was extremely elaborate and imposing with scrollwork and mock organ pipes. It needed a team of eight horses to move it.

As soon as the second performance was over everything was swiftly on its way back to the station for the overnight journey to Colchester. Large crowds watched the proceedings late into the night and a group of Indians gathered at the entrance to the station caused a huge stir.

The success of the Southend show underlines the fame and popularity of Buffalo Bill and his show. The town was at that time in its heyday as a holiday resort and there were plenty of alternative amusements on offer. The Kursaal, for example, had opened just two years earlier as part of one of the world's first purpose-built amusement parks.

The main building – known as the Kursaal Palace – had a circus, theatre, ballroom, arcade,

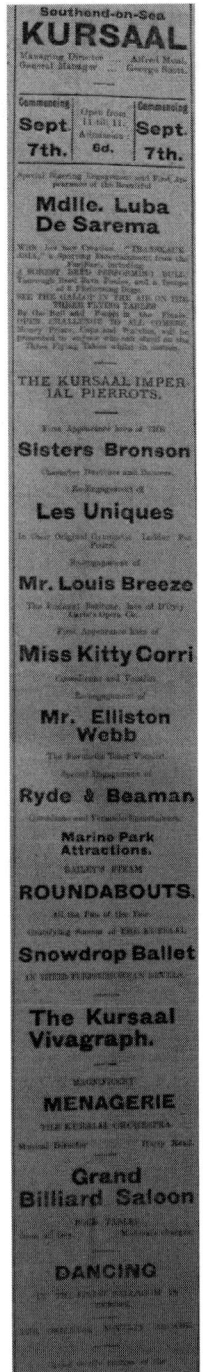

Right: Kursaal newspaper advertisement for the week Buffalo Bill visited Southend

dining hall and billiard room. Not to be outdone by the Wild West, the circus that week was offering 'marvellous bare back riders', 'graceful equestrian acts' and to compete with Buffalo Bill's bucking broncos it featured Barney the bucking mule.

Also performing at the Kursaal was Mademoiselle Luba De Sarema with a show called 'Transkaukasia' which featured a 'forest bred performing bull', thoroughbred ponies and a troupe of performing dogs. The finale of the show was 'the gallop in the air on three flying tables' by the bull and the ponies but what this could possibly have entailed is now sadly lost.

The Wild West arrived at Colchester North station early next morning, Friday 4th September and began unloading about 5am. Despite the early hour many people came to see the arrival which was said to be a sight in itself. Among the attractions were the eight feet two inch Egyptian giant and the two feet high Princess Hawa. The performers immediately headed for the showground at Reed Hall, about a mile away and a procession of Indians going up North Hill caused great excitement. The group included several chiefs 'of dignified bearing' as The Ipswich *Evening Star* newspaper remarked. The paper was amused to note that among them was a chief called Lone Bear but the crowds that flocked round him afforded very little solitude.

The roads to Reed Hall were jammed with carriages, cyclists and pedestrians and the side shows were doing good business early in the day. To ensure security a New York detective by the name of C.C. Murphy had been employed to travel with the show. He'd been called into action earlier in the tour when Buffalo Bill's valet suddenly disappeared with several of his jewels including a diamond studded pin which had been presented by King Edward VII. After three days Murphy tracked down the culprit and recovered the jewels. The thief got six months' hard labour.

Chief Lone Bear – the Evening Star newspaper was amused to note that, despite his name, the crowds in Colchester afforded him very little solitude

The afternoon performance was attended by Sir William Gatacre and his wife and several officers from the nearby barracks. General Gatacre was a distinguished soldier who had commanded an army division at the Battle of Omdurman in the Sudan under the command of General Kitchener. Returning home, he was appointed General Officer Commanding Eastern District based at Colchester. At the outbreak of the Second Boer War he served in Africa where he suffered a humiliating defeat at the Battle of Stormberg. This dented the high reputation he had earned after his victory at Omdurman

General Sir William Gatacre

but nonetheless on his return home he was re-appointed to his old command in Colchester. His appearance at the Wild West show prompted a salute delivered with military precision by Buffalo Bill and his horsemen. The *Evening Star* reporter was impressed by Bill's skill in shooting from horseback. The feat was doubly wonderful, he thought, in view of Bill's age (he was fifty seven) and the fact that he had to wear glasses.

After the performance the side shows were again thronged. Colchester being a military town, one attraction of particular interest was the 'blue-skinned man' who was a former soldier. He had been serving with the 17th Lancers British cavalry regiment when his horse fell on him and after a few months a blue spot appeared on his chest.

The colour gradually spread over his whole body. A medical examination concluded the accident had damaged a valve in his heart causing a discolouration of the blood.

The evening performance started promptly at 8pm and went well until an hour or so later a violent storm erupted over the showground. Although the spectators were sheltered, the torrential rain caused huge problems for the performers as the arena was open and the grass became extremely slippery. Wet grass was dangerous for performers galloping at full speed on horseback. Earlier in the season, in Manchester, Buffalo Bill himself had fallen victim. He had ridden out at the start of the show to introduce his congress of rough riders when his horse shied at a piece of scenery being moved, reared up and unseated him. The horse slipped again and fell onto Bill's right foot crushing it. As a result, he was unable to ride for several weeks but, determined not to disappoint the public, performed while being driven in an open carriage. The conditions during the Colchester show were made more difficult by the fact that there were two slopes in the arena but even so the show continued without incident accompanied according to one reporter by 'vivid lightning flashes and peals of thunder'.

As the performance ended the same reporter noted: 'It was pitiable to see the horsemen who had afforded such pleasure to such a vast a crowd leaving for the railway station drenched to the skin; but all showed the utmost "grit" and cheerfulness'. Many were observed to be singing as they rode along.

The spectators fared little better; many had long distances to travel by pony and trap or bicycle and by the time they got home many were said to look as if they had been pulled from a pond and hundreds of ladies' dresses were ruined. From Colchester the show moved to Ipswich and then on through East Anglia.

The weather remained poor but Bill battled on until finally, in October, it got the better of him. Writing home to his sister from Bradford he described 'Fifty hours of the worst cold rain and wind storms I have ever experienced in all my life. We stood it off for forty three hours but had to give up and tonight have lost our first show of this season. We commenced pulling at 8.15. At 8.37 a house adjoining our big top was blown down and fell on our seats. Had we had an audience in, they would have been killed so we were lucky not to attempt a show. I have been cold and wet since early Monday morning it's now Tuesday eve 10.45.'

The season ended at Burton on Trent on October 23rd. Between the final two shows Bill hosted a lunch for the company and guests including top managers from the Barnum and Bailey organisation. After the meal he gave a speech in which he complimented everyone for their loyalty and uncomplaining work throughout months of rain and mud. He hoped to see many of the familiar faces back in the arena in the spring. He added: 'You are about to depart to your various homes, a journey which takes you many thousands of miles apart. I am in hope that you will occasionally remember the season of 1903 in good old loyal England where we have been treated so kindly by everyone we have come into contact with'.

After 333 performances the company dispersed to their various homes around the world; the American contingent boarded the *Lucania* at Liverpool for New York. Once there Bill set out for his ranch in Wyoming to spend the winter. The horses, cattle and equipment remained behind at Etruria in Staffordshire, the former estate of the pottery maker, Josiah Wedgewood. A few cowboys also stayed behind on full pay to care for the animals and maintain equipment.

10. The Final Tour – Chelmsford and Ilford

Bill returned to Liverpool on the *Lucania* in April 1904 ready to resume his tour. Publicity billed this as his parting salute to Great Britain and declared the show would positively never be seen there again. People were urged to: 'See it NOW or NEVER'. The season began at Stoke on Trent on April 25th. The show was substantially the same as the previous year with some changes. Gone was the Battle of San Juan Hill to be replaced by the reintroduction of the Battle of the Little Big Horn or 'Custer's Last Stand'. This may have been due to the fact that, although different towns were being visited this year, many were close to those which saw performances the previous season and the management wanted to keep the entertainment fresh. Young Sitting Bull – said to be the son of the famous chief – played his father in the battle and the marksman Johnny Baker, wearing a long blond wig, took the part of General Custer. This section of the show was heavily promoted in 1904 and Major Burke distributed leaflets reading:

THE BATTLE OF THE LITTLE BIG HORN
The Awful Reality of Furious Conflict and Massacre in Savage Warfare
Presented with Perfect Historical Accuracy of Detail
Introducing 800 Indian Chiefs, Braves and Warriors, Soldiers, Scouts and Horses
With Every Accessory of Arms, Accoutrement and Savage Decoration,
Whose Inconceivably Overpowering, Apotheosis of Mortal Combat
Is the Illustrious Tableaux of
CUSTER'S LAST STAND AND HEROIC FALL.
The World Will Never See Its Like Again!
Everything Presented is Realism Itself

Also new this year was Carter the Cowboy Cyclist who performed a thrilling stunt – cycling at high speed down a ramp from a platform around forty feet high and then leaping across a gap forty feet wide to land on another ramp the other side. This was a dangerous act and a week after appearing in Essex Carter suffered a nasty accident while appearing at Mansfield in Nottinghamshire. His bicycle appeared to twist in the air which threw him off course and he crashed, hitting one of the poles which carried the electric arc lamps. He was knocked unconscious and suffered cuts to the head. So dangerous was this stunt that accidents were not unusual and there was said to be more than one 'Carter' who could fill in should the original be hurt. In fact, as the sideshow magician Charles Eldridge Griffin noted in his book, the whole show was dangerous. The previous year one of the Mexican riders had been thrown from his horse and killed. Griffin wrote: 'Every time (the performers) enter the arena, especially the bucking horse act, they practically take their lives in their hands'. The 1903 show programme noted that every day up to half a dozen cowboys were laid up as a result

Chief Flying Hawk was a prominent performer in Buffalo Bill's Wild West and had actually fought in the Battle of the Little Big Horn. A re-enactment of the battle featured in the 1904 show. He died, reportedly from starvation, in 1931 at the age of seventy seven on a reservation in South Dakota.

of their battle with the broncos.

Another new addition for this season was an Imperial Japanese Troupe who gave a display of ancient and modern war drills.

Their arrival had brought the potential for friction with the Russian Cossacks since the Russo-Japanese war had begun in February but apparently the two groups got on well together.

The Wild West travelled to Chelmsford from Wimbledon arriving at 5am on June 19th. But as this was a Sunday there was no show that day. Two performances were scheduled for the next day and as usual the advance party had ensured maximum publicity with posters, adverts and articles in the *Essex Chronicle*. On June 10th the paper declared: 'A great event in the entertainment line is approaching which the people of Chelmsford and district will not regret if they respond *en masse*.' The paper went on to

Newspaper advertisement for the Wild West's performance in Chelmsford. From the front page of the Essex Chronicle, June 17th 1904, three days before the show

quote at length the words of the famous actor, Sir Henry Irving, who said: 'No circus can approximate its actuality. It is impossible to escape the thrill of intense action. The enthusiasm of the multitude goes with him (Buffalo Bill)'.

A week later, three days before the show, the paper was equally enthusiastic:

'Buffalo Bill's Wild West has never been to this town before and can never return ... (it) is not a circus but consists of genuine representatives of different races and nations, associated with perfection of horsemanship and military skill.'

The advance publicity worked; the Great Eastern Railway put on extra trains and cheap return fares were offered from most stations in the county.

The Chelmsford Show was sited on fourteen acres at Goldlay Meadows, off Baddow Road, which had recently hosted the Essex Agricultural Show. Large crowds were attracted to the entrances on Sunday morning but were disappointed not to be let in. The newspapers had originally announced that parts of the showground would be open to the public outside the hours of church services. But the show's managers said they had been asked not open and not wishing to upset anyone had agreed to the request. This led to some recrimination with both the showground owners and the tenant who had sub-let it denying having made any such request. The disappointed crowds had to be content with watching the extraordinary sight of cowboys, Indians, Japanese, Cossacks, Mexicans and Arabs walking the streets of Chelmsford. According to the *Essex Chronicle* their 'gay attire' and 'jaunty airs' created great interest.

The two shows on Monday went off without a hitch. Between eight and nine thousand people attended the afternoon performance and all the cheaper seats were sold out. The evening performance attracted an even bigger crowd put at 11,000. The scale of the event meant that it received coverage across the county and the *Barking and Ilford Advertiser* reported: 'The fame of Col. Cody and his rough riders drawn from all parts of the world has a strong hold on all classes of the community, and it was not surprising that on the occasion of the first visit of this famous entertainment to the county town the assemblage from far and near should be so large.'

One of the Wild West's Indian performers

The *Essex Chronicle's* reporter was overcome by the spectacle: 'The show itself is like that which caused such a sensation in London. One can hardly enumerate all the features in a newspaper report.' He added: '... the congress of rough riders of the world which Col. Cody himself introduces, is as instructive as it is extraordinary. Expert military feats are also performed while Buffalo Bill and Johnny Baker manifest marksmanship which must be seen to be believed.' The friendly relations between the Japanese and the Cossacks, he thought, were particularly interesting given that they would soon be called up by their respective armies to fight each other.

The Wild West was soon on its way, by Tuesday morning it had arrived in Ilford and was firmly established on the Kingsfield Estate, off Ilford Lane. The advance publicity machine had been in action again supplying whatever facts and figures the local press demanded. The *Ilford Guardian* was particularly impressed by the size of the transport operation: 'On Tuesday next, there will arrive at Ilford the most remarkable train-freight that has ever been brought here by the Great Eastern Railway Company. Three quarters of a mile of trains will bring Buffalo Bill's Wild West Show …. The first section of eighteen cars will be 972 feet in length; the second section of seventeen cars will measure 918 and the third section of fourteen cars will cover 756 feet. These figures will give a small idea of the magnitude of the show to be provided for the entertainment of Ilfordians and all who care to come from far and near.'

The publicity did its job and the show was a huge attraction with people pouring into the town from far and wide. Throughout the day there was great interest in the show's exotic cast. During the show itself there was said to be undiminished admiration for the horsemanship and the animals on display. The appearance of Carter the cowboy cyclist was a sensation as he leapt successfully through space firing a pistol in mid-air.

From time to time local dignitaries were invited to ride in the Deadwood stagecoach as it was attacked by Indians. At Earl's Court during the show's first visit to England in 1887 the coach had carried no less than four Kings – of Denmark, Saxony, Greece and Belgium plus the Prince of Wales. On this occasion the passengers during the afternoon show were less distinguished but caused no less of a stir with the news of what happened being carried by newspapers around the country.

The excitement started with the arrival of a telegram from Major Burke addressed to Buffalo Bill warning him that a strong contingent of 'Indians' had left for his camp on the one-eighteen train from London's Liverpool Street station. It transpired that the 'Indians' were a group of girls currently performing in the

Broadway musical 'The Prince of Pilsen' at the Shaftsbury Theatre. The show had opened the previous month to enthusiastic reviews. *The Evening News* reported: 'There is not a dull moment from the minute the curtain rises till it finally falls …. Old theatre-goers said … that they had seldom seen so perfectly drilled a chorus before on any English stage…. Never was the applause so enthusiastic.'

Shortly after the telegram from Major Burke, another arrived from the girls themselves promising: 'If we cannot shout louder than your Indians your cowboys can lynch us'.

This was, no doubt, a carefully prepared stunt by the show's publicity team but it succeeded perfectly. As news of the girls' arrival spread a large crowd gathered to see them. They were led by Camille Clifford, a Belgian born actress who had travelled from America with the show and was famous for her beauty and eighteen inch 'wasp' waist. Miss Clifford and three other girls from the show were

Camille Clifford: Famous for her beauty and 'wasp' waist

invited to ride in the Deadwood stagecoach.

As it careered around the arena it was duly attacked by a party of Indians and as ever rescued by the timely arrival of a group of cowboys.

As the stage came to a halt Buffalo Bill himself was on hand to help the girls alight. Miss Clifford was apparently carried away by the excitement of the occasion: 'Colonel', she declared, 'we've had a lovely time'. Then she added: 'Oh is he not just too sweet' and, in the words of one newspaper report, 'clasping the silver-haired colonel about the neck, she kissed him with the innocent fervour of a long-lost daughter.' At that the other girls followed suit causing Bill to blush furiously. The Indians howled with delight and the cowboys cheered.

It wasn't the first time Camille Clifford had been in the news for her flamboyant behaviour. A month earlier the show's chorus girls had been at the centre of a controversy when they were accused of winking at members of the audience. The girls denied the charge and Miss Clifford told the *Daily Express*: 'On Broadway they want us to look light-hearted and happy and lively. There we are fired out if we don't smile. But we never smile at individuals; we smile at the ceiling. The stout old lady in the box gets just as much of our attention as her handsome son'.

The relentless tour continued and the Wild West left Ilford for the next day's performances in St Albans. Later it headed north before crossing into Scotland for two months. Then it was south through Lancashire and Yorkshire before the final performance at Hanley in Staffordshire on Friday October 21st 1904. The audience was huge, many drawn, as the *Staffordshire Sentinel* noted, 'because they once again wished to look on the face and figure of one of the most wonderful men of his day …. The audience, as soon as they saw him coming on his beautiful brown charger, which he handled so splendidly, raised a large cheer enough to please the veteran no end.' After the show everything was loaded onto the three trains for the last time and taken to Liverpool where the steam ship *Campania* was waiting to take it to New York.

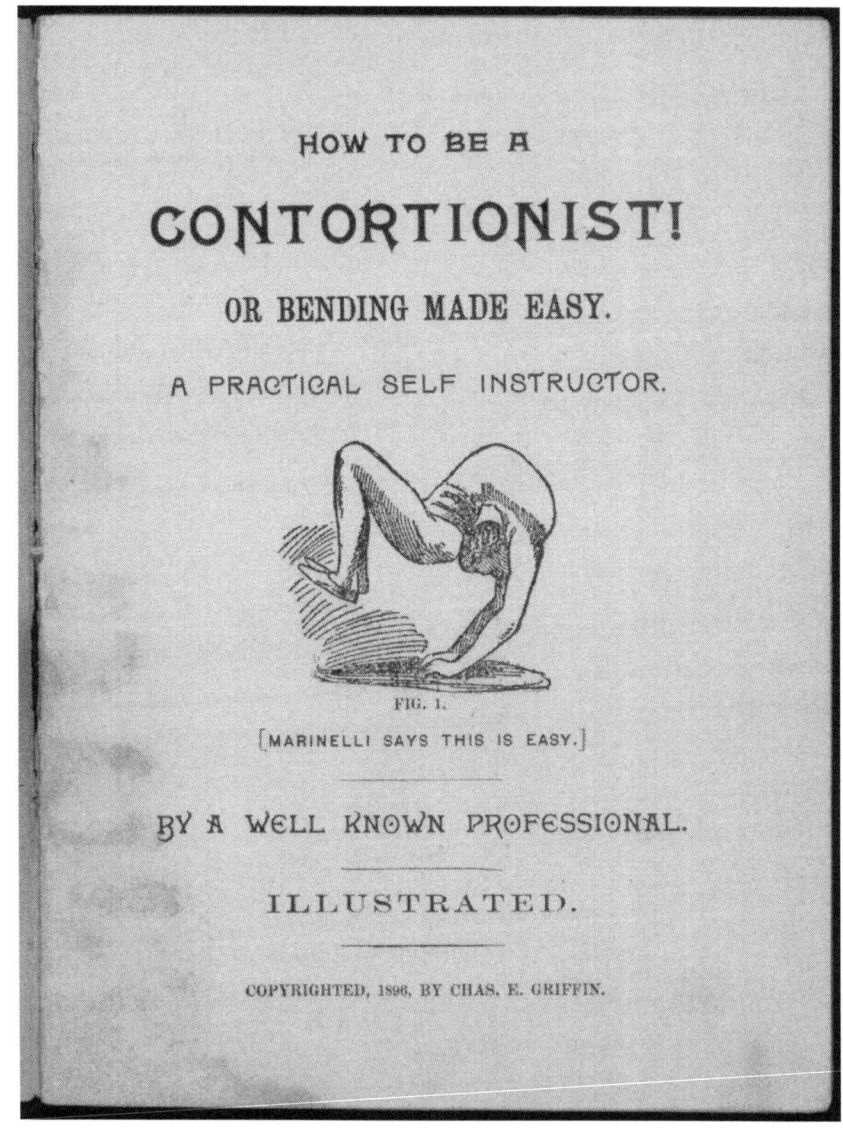

Among those appearing with Buffalo Bill in Essex was Charles Eldridge Griffin. He was a man of many talents – author, comedian, conjuror, contortionist and publisher. Among his numerous books was this one on how to be a contortionist.

11. The End of the Trail

The 1904 season would be the last time the Wild West was seen in Britain and it was a spectacular success. Charles Eldridge Griffin wrote that it had 'been the best in the history of the show, and members of the Wild West, from the highest to the lowest (bade) farewell to merry old England with keen regrets and sincere good wishes for the prosperity of her hospitable people, the fairest and squarest country in the world to a stranger.'

The tour had visited more than 130 towns and cities and covered more than 4,100 miles by rail and a further 440 miles from railway sidings to showgrounds and back again. The weather during 1904 had been much better than the previous year and the show had been more profitable. Huge crowds had been drawn to the shows from a wide area round about and as well as spending money on admission they had also brought trade to restaurants, hotels, pubs, cabs and shops. Major Burke declared: 'Colonel Cody and the Wild West are public benefactors and bring money out of secret hiding places and put it into circulation. There is always enough money in any country, and if it is in circulation, times are good. If it is kept locked up, times will be hard. Therefore, the man or institution who keeps it in circulation is certainly a friend of the people and should be welcomed as such.'

Bill returned to his home in Wyoming. His relationship with his wife, aggravated by his long absences, had been difficult for years and he filed for divorce. The court heard lurid accusations, including a claim that Cody's wife had tried to poison him and of his drinking, unreasonable behaviour and 'intimacy with other women'. In the end the judge threw out the case declaring incompatibility was not grounds for divorce.

Buffalo Bill performing in 1907

The following year, after the unsuccessful court case and beset by financial problems, Bill returned to continental Europe for another 'farewell' tour, including a three-month season in Paris. He had been reluctant to go but James Bailey, who now owned seventy five per cent of the Wild West, wanted it out of the country so it did not compete with his circus interests.

In 1906 when the show had reached Rome news arrived that Bailey had died. His shares passed to his wife who planned to sell them but until that happened sole responsibility for the show rested with Bill.

The Bailey estate began to sell its assets and Gordon W. Lillie – Pawnee Bill – Cody's old friend who had helped procure Indians for the first Wild West production stepped in. Lillie had run his own Wild

West show and in 1908 the two shows were combined and set out under the name 'Buffalo Bill's Wild West company with Pawnee Bill's Great Far East'. Despite its unpromising title, the show was a success and the two men dispensed with Bailey's circus and freak show elements to concentrate on its Wild West aspects.

In 1908 Buffalo Bill merged his show with the Wild West show run by his old friend Pawnee Bill. This picture was taken three years earlier and shows Pawnee Bill's interpretation of the death of Custer at the Battle of the Little Big Horn

Although the 1910 season was promoted as Buffalo Bill's farewell American tour, he set out again in 1911. This season was poor; the show lost money wherever it went, with audiences restricted by bad weather. The 1912 tour was billed as the 'final farewell'. Bill was well into his sixties by now, his hair was thinning and he had taken to wearing a hair-piece in the arena to maintain the illusion of youth. The 1912 tour was profitable but Cody was losing money on other business ventures and needed cash to repay creditors. At that point he received an offer from an unscrupulous businessman named Harry Tammen who part owned the *Denver Post* newspaper and a circus called Sells-Floto. He lent Bill $20,000 (worth nearly a third of a million dollars today) to keep him solvent.

Although Pawnee Bill was unhappy with the arrangement the tour continued but the weather was again bad and they lost money. Half the Indians deserted and to make matters worse, Cody was suffering from an enlarged prostate which made it painful

Buffalo Bill in 1913

for him to ride a horse so he performed his shooting act while being pulled in an open buggy. When the show arrived in Denver Tammen was waiting to call in his loan. Neither Cody or Pawnee Bill had the money and Tammen sent in the bailiffs. The Wild West – animals, wagons, props and all the equipment was auctioned in Denver on September 15th 1913.

Bill returned home to Wyoming and became involved in the growing film industry producing eight short films based on his life, again made as authentic as possible by the use of actual locations and some of the actual participants.

In 1915 he was forced to tour with the Sells-Floto Circus as part of his loan agreement with Harry Tammen. Bill arrived home exhausted having given 366 performances in 183 days covering nearly 17,000 miles. But he had recovered sufficiently by the next year to set out again, this time with his wife with whom he had been reconciled. But Bill had had enough. After a tense meeting with Tammen during which Bill occasionally reached for one of the pistols that lay on the table between them he was released from his contract at the end of the 1916 season.

Still short of money, Bill joined the '101 Ranch Wild West' another travelling show which also took on Johnny Baker. Bill's health continued to decline and sometimes he needed Johnny's help just to mount his horse but as soon as he entered the arena the years fell away and he rode like the hero of old. Bill's final appearance came in Portsmouth, Virginia, on November 11th 1916.

He had planned to return to the show the following year but in January, while on a visit to a Colorado sanatorium to take a mineral water cure, he collapsed. Buffalo Bill was taken to his sister's home in Denver and died there in his wife's arms, aged seventy, on January 10th 1917.

His funeral rivalled the scale and colour of his old Wild West show. After much controversy a grave-site was chosen on Lookout Mountain near Denver and among the 3,000 motor cars and hundreds of horse drawn carriages making their way up the mountain on June 3rd 1917 were gaudily painted wagons from the Sells-Floto Circus. The crowd was put at 25,000 and those wishing to pay their last respects had to queue for two hours to walk past the coffin. Buffalo Bill was laid to rest to the sound of an eleven-gun salute.

Buffalo Bill's grave on Lookout Mountain near Denver, Colorado

Shortly after his death, Annie Oakley paid this tribute: 'I never saw him in any situation that changed his natural attitude a scintilla. None could possibly tell the difference between his reception of a band of cowboys and the train of an emperor ... He was probably the guest of more people in diverse circumstances than any man living. But a tepee or a palace were all the same to him, and so were their inhabitants....His heart never left the great West. Whenever the day's work was done, he could always be found sitting alone watching the sinking sun, and at every opportunity he took the trail back to his old home. The sun setting over the mountain will pay its daily tribute to the resting place of the last of the great builders of the West...'

Annie Oakley herself died of pernicious anaemia in 1926 at the age of sixty six. Her husband, Frank Butler, distraught at his wife's death, stopped eating and died eighteen days later.

Despite the black crepe and flags at half-mast when news of Nate Salsbury's death reached Buffalo Bill as he prepared to perform at Olympia in 1902, it emerged later that all had not been well between the two men. In an unpublished memoir, Salsbury revealed himself as a bitter man who believed he alone was the creator of the Wild West show and responsible for its success. He regarded Buffalo Bill as a drunk who had visited the homes of foreign dignitaries while under the influence and on one occasion had hardly been able to get into his carriage while accompanied by a lady who was 'manifestly not Mrs Cody'. Salsbury's bitterness encompassed many of Buffalo Bill's closest associates who he dismissed as hanging on to Bill's coat tails for their sustenance. Of the publicity genius John Burke, he conceded: 'I do not believe there is another man in the world who could have covered as much space in the newspapers of the day as John Burke has done'. But there was a sting in the tail: '... and I do not believe there is another man in the world in his position that would have the gall to exploit himself at the expense of the show as much as John Burke.' Burke himself died in 1917, just three months after Buffalo Bill, at the age of seventy five.

Of the other major characters in the extraordinary story of Buffalo Bill's Wild West ….

Wild Bill Hickock died in 1876, shot while playing cards at the age of thirty nine.

Texas **Jack Omohundro** married **Giuseppina Morlacchi** after they starred with Buffalo Bill in 'Scouts of the Plains'. Their marriage was tragically short lived. Jack died of pneumonia in 1880 at the age of just thirty three. Giuseppina survived for only another six years before dying of cancer. She was thirty nine.

Ned Buntline also died in 1886 – there is uncertainty over his date of birth, he was either sixty three or sixty five.

Captain Adam Bogardus – 'Champion Pigeon Shot of America' – died at the age of seventy eight in 1913.

Buffalo Bill's **wife Louisa** died in 1921, aged seventy eight, and was buried next to her husband.

Red Shirt, the chief who met the Prince of Wales in 1887, died in 1925 at the age of seventy seven and is buried on the Pine Ridge Reservation in South Dakota.

The irascible **Doc Carver** survived until 1927.

Johnny Baker – The Cowboy Kid – died of cancer in 1931 at the age of sixty two.

Lone Bear, who was among the Indians who caused a sensation when they walked up North Hill in Colchester in 1903, continued performing with Wild West shows until 1935 and visited Europe several times. He disappeared from history and the last record of him comes in the 1940 census at Pine Ridge Reservation.

Gordon W Lillie – Pawnee Bill – died in his sleep in 1942 at the age of eighty one.

And finally ... **Camille Clifford**, the Belgian-born Broadway actress who caused such a stir when she kissed Buffalo Bill during the 1904 show in Ilford, outlived them all. She retired from the stage and married soon after her Ilford appearance but her husband was killed in the First World War. She married again and later ran a stable of successful racehorses in England. She died in 1971 at the age of eighty five.

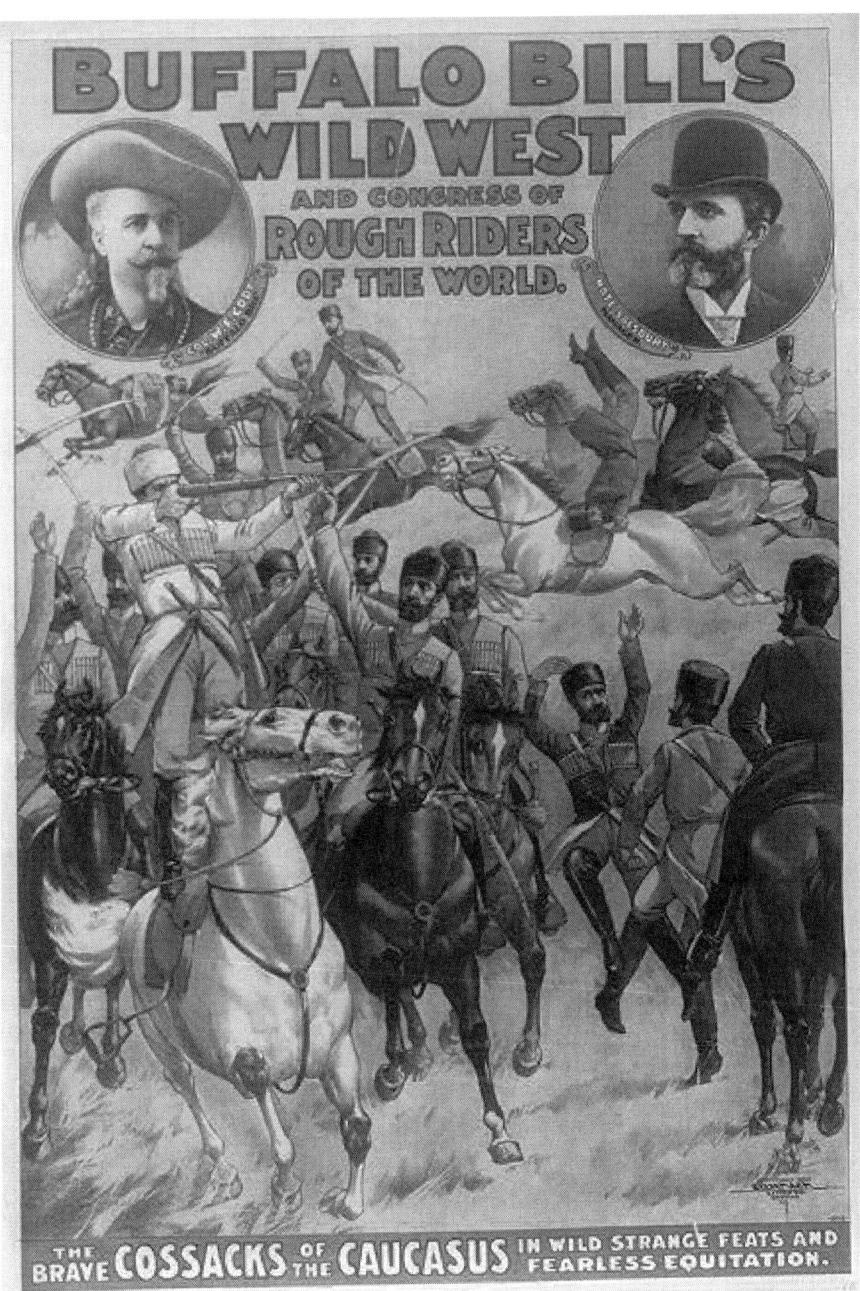

Poster advertising Buffalo Bill's Wild West from around the time the show visited Essex

Selected Bibliography

Adams, Bluford, *E Pluribus Barnum: The Great Showman and the Making of U.S. Popular Culture,* University of Minnesota Press, Minneapolis, 1997.

Bridger, Bobby, *Buffalo Bill and Sitting Bull: Inventing the Wild West,* University of Texas Press, Austin, 2002.

Carter, Robert A., *Buffalo Bill Cody: The Man Behind the Legend,* Castle, Edison NJ, 2005.

Cody, Louisa Frederici, *Memories of Buffalo Bill,* D. Appleton & Co., New York, 1919.

Cody, William F., *The Life of Hon. William F. Cody, Known as Buffalo Bill,* University of Nebraska Press, Lincoln, 2011.

Cody, William F., *The Wild West in England,* University of Nebraska Press, Lincoln, 2012.

Feest, Christian F., *Indians and Europe,* University of Nebraska Press, Lincoln, 1999.

Foote, Stella Adelyne, *Letters from Buffalo Bill,* Foote Publishing, Billings, Montana, 1954.

Gallop, Alan, *Buffalo Bill's British Wild West,* The History Press, Stroud, 2009.

Griffin, Charles Eldridge, *Four Years in Europe With Buffalo Bill,* University of Nebraska Press, Lincoln, 2010.

Griffin, Charles Eldridge, *How to Be a Contortionist, or, Bending Made Easy,* Charles E. Griffin, New York, 1886.

Maddra, Sam A. *Hostiles?: The Lakota Ghost Dance and Buffalo Bill's Wild West,* University of Oklahoma Press, Norman, 2006.

McMurty, Larry, *The Colonel and Little Missy,* Simon and Schuster, New York, 2006.

Monaghan, Jay, *The Great Rascal Ned Buntline,* Little, Brown & Co., Boston, 1952.

Noble, James, *Around the Coast with Buffalo Bill: The Wild West in Yorkshire and Lincolnshire,* Hutton, Beverley, 1999.

Russell, Don, *The Lives and Legends of Buffalo Bill,* University of

Oklahoma Press, Norman, 1960.

Standing Bear, Luther, *My People the Sioux,* University of Nebraska Press, Lincoln, 2006.

Warren, Louis S. *Buffalo Bill's America: William Cody and the Wild West Show,* Alfred A. Knopf, New York, 2005.

Weybright, Victor and Sell, Henry, *Buffalo Bill and the Wild West,* Hamish Hamilton, London, 1956.

Wilson, R.L. with Martin, Greg, *Buffalo Bill's Wild West – An American Legend,* Greenhill Books, London, 1998.

About the Author

David Dunford was born in Chelmsford and attended the University of Essex, graduating with a degree in Government in 1972. He joined *Essex County Newspapers* in Colchester as a reporter and later became an assistant editor.

In 1978 he moved to the BBC in London where he worked in the Radio Newsroom writing news bulletins for all domestic outlets. He also wrote for *Yesterday* and *Today in Parliament* as well as writing and broadcasting on finance for radio, television and the BBC World Service.

He later became Editor of the BBC General News Service, responsible for providing news and current affairs for BBC English local radio stations and BBC Scotland, Wales and Northern Ireland. He was also a member of a European Broadcasting Union working party on local radio in Europe. In 2003 he was Editor of all BBC local radio and regional television coverage of the second Gulf War.

After taking early retirement from the BBC he became a visiting lecturer in radio journalism at the University of the Arts in London.

In 2014 he returned to Essex University to study for an MA in History which he was awarded with distinction.

In 2017 his first book *FULL CIRCLE the Rise, Fall and Rise of Horse Racing in Chelmsford* was published.

Essex Hundred Publications Titles Available

BATTLEFIELD ESSEX
2000 years of conflict in Essex
ISBN 9780993108341 £8.99

THE ESSEX HUNDRED HISTORIES
From the Roman sacking of Colchester to Ford's modern day wind turbines each chapter reflects the diversity of the county as well as showing the role Essex has played in the nation's development.
ISBN: 9780993108310 £9.99

THE ESSEX HUNDRED
The history of the county of Essex described in 100 poems and supported with historical notes and illustrations.
A unique book written by Essex poets covering 2,000 years of county history.
ISBN: 9780955229503 £7.99

LONDON'S METROPOLITAN ESSEX
Events and Personalities, from Essex in London, which shaped the nation's history.
ISBN 9780955229558 £12.99

THEY DID THEIR DUTY, ESSEX FARM
Never Forgotten
Andrew Summers

A book that tells the story of Essex Farm, a First World War cemetery in Belgium, that will forever bear the county name, and its connections to the Essex Regiment.
ISBN 9780955229596 RRP £9.99

THE ESSEX HUNDRED CHILDREN'S COLOURING AND ACTIVITY BOOK

The Colouring and Activity Book is another title from the Essex Hundred family aimed at children and part written by children. The book includes not only Essex information but pictures to colour in, word searches, puzzles and questions.
ISBN: 9780955229534 £4.99

THE NUMBERS HAD TO TALLY
by Kazimierz Szmauz
A World War II Extraordinary Tale of Survival
ISBN: 9780955229572 RRP £8.99

ONCE UPON A TIME IN SOUTHEND AND DISTRICT

Over ninety popular local newspaper cartoons from 1936 – 1939 with original captions and added text that could be as relevant today as when they were first published.
ISBN 9780993108396 RRP £9.99

**Digital Editions available for
Essex Farm
The Numbers Had to Tally
L33 and other stories from WWI**

Essex Hundred Publications

Books written, designed and printed in Essex.
Available from bookshops, book wholesalers,
direct from the publisher or
online www.essex100.com

Chief Iron Tail pictured during the 1904 tour which visited Chelmsford and Ilford.